a
heart
to
teach

a heart to teach

Quiet Times & Tools for Excelling in the Children's Ministry

edited by
Thomas Jones & Kelly Petre

DPI
DISCIPLESHIP
PUBLICATIONS
INTERNATIONAL

A Heart to Teach
© 2000 by Discipleship Publications International
One Merrill Street, Woburn, Mass. 01801
www.dpibooks.org

Printed in the United States of America

Book Design: Chad Crossland

ISBN: 1-57782-135-1

To the team of parents, educators, artists, writers and editors—many of them volunteers and all of them disciples—who were used by God to miraculously produce the Kingdom Kids Curriculum in only a few short years.

Our children and their heavenly Father thank you.

Contents

PART 2: TOOLS AND RESOURCES

Acknowledgments

In the summer of 1999, with the Kingdom Kids Curriculum project more than half finished, the advisory committee for the curriculum met in Hartford, Connecticut, to consider what follow-up was needed upon completion of the curriculum. The idea that received the most enthusiastic support was the development of a resource book for disciples who are about to enter their time of service in the children's ministry. Other projects, including books for children and parents, were also planned, but the book for those who would serve in children's ministry was given top priority.

Early in the year 2000, I asked Kelly Petre, who had just joined the DPI editorial staff, to oversee the development of this project. Kelly met with Amby Murphy who had served for three years on the staff of the Kingdom Kids Curriculum project and who had developed a possible outline for this book. Additional meetings were held with Larry Wood and Sheila Jones, who provided valuable ideas.

Chapters were once again requested from many of the dedicated members of the advisory committee, plus others committed to children's ministry who had come to our attention during the development of the curriculum. Additional material written for the curriculum was taken and adapted, and we are grateful for all those who made these original contributions.

Kelly made all the initial assignments for the new material and then turned his attention to another project for which he was needed. I worked with my wife, Sheila, Kim Hanson and Lisa Morris on the final editorial work.

Very special thanks are extended to Al Baird and Gordon and Theresa Ferguson. These three carry many heavy ministry loads, but are totally committed to planting faith in the next generation. They all graciously agreed to contribute important pieces to this volume. This has truly been a team effort—as it should be in the kingdom! Our prayer is that it will be used to inspire many to teach and serve our children excellently and to build the faith of our children.

Thomas Jones
Editor in Chief
Discipleship Publications International

Introduction
SENDING A MESSAGE

Al Baird • Los Angeles, USA

"Children are the living message we send to a time we will not see."[1] This quotation, by sociologist Neil Postman, is at the same time both exhilarating and sobering. It's exhilarating for disciples because we can pass on the living heart of the gospel message to succeeding generations by first passing it on to our children. It's sobering because if it does not become real to them, we will fail to pass the message on. So the crucial question for the modern day movement of God is, Will we succeed in passing the gospel on to our children?

The Importance of Parents

This book has been written to help you prepare for your service in the children's ministry of the church. The things you will read here will impress on you the fact that your work with our children is vital and needs to be done spiritually and excellently. But let me begin with some comments about parents, first, because that is what many of you are; and second, because as a children's ministry worker, one of your key roles is to encourage parents to be faithful in their calling.

Perhaps the greatest promise to parents in the Bible is Proverbs 22:6, "Train a child in the way he should go, and when he is old he will not turn from it." But it is a conditional promise: There must be training by the parents. You, as Kingdom Kids teachers, can offer significant help. Schoolteachers and coaches can also make a big difference in children's lives. But in reality, no one has as much influence as parents, who normally have eighteen years to train their children. Parenting is the purest form of discipling. Seldom will you ever get as much time to mold and shape another person as a parent gets with a child. Jesus said in Luke 6:40, "A student is not above his teacher, but everyone who is fully trained will be like his teacher." A child, in fact, will be trained by his parents, and he or she will usually become like them, for better or for worse. Exactly what a child turns out to be will depend on the kind of training the parents give.

1. Neil Postman, *The Disappearance of Childhood* (New York: Vintage Books, 1982, 1994) xi.

Training is not just instructing. Who you are screams louder than what you teach. Children, as well as adults, learn primarily by example. If what is taught is different from what is modeled, the *example* will usually win out over the *teaching.* Children, especially teens, rebel against hypocrisy.

My wife, Gloria, had the opportunity to teach a parenting class with our daughter Staci (herself the mother of three daughters). In preparation for the class, Gloria asked Staci what primarily stood out about our parenting as she was growing up. Staci said that what was most important was that we, as her parents, were the same people at home with her and her two sisters as we were away from home. This answer was encouraging to us because we had prayed and worked hard to set this example.

Gloria and I do a lot of family counseling. A counseling appointment became perhaps the saddest I have ever experienced when a teenage boy looked his mother and father in the eyes and said, "You don't have anything in your life that I want." To train a child, first we must each be the person we want him or her to become. If a parent is a lukewarm Christian, that parent is most likely sending his or her child to hell! It would be better for a parent to be an atheist than to be a lukewarm disciple, because at least if a parent doesn't pretend to be a disciple, then the true picture of a disciple has not been tainted.

Denominational Christianity is a turnoff for most kids today because it's much too watered down and way too comfortable. Biblical Christianity is built on sacrifice, the sacrifices of putting God and his kingdom first (Matthew 6:33) and giving up everything (Luke 14:33). This radical lifestyle inspires our children. As they grow older, parents face the temptation to become more cautious and comfortable. Nevertheless, they must avoid settling in and putting something other than God first. It's easy to give lip service to the right priorities, but children see and know what their parents' priorities really are.

Looking back, I believe that what made the biggest impact on our girls was my decision to give up my fifteen-year career as a research scientist in order to join the ministry staff. They saw the sacrifice, felt the insecurity of having their parents begin new careers in their forties, and experienced the incredible blessings of God as a result of our leap of faith. All three of our daughters today are strong disciples, happily married to strong disciples, and are also on the ministry staff.

God has blessed our family in incredible ways, far beyond anything we ever imagined. But we are not meant to be unique. We have simply claimed his promises—the same promises that he wants every disciple with children to claim.

If you are a parent, as you work in the children's ministry, let this become a time to be more deeply convicted about the role you as a parent play in shaping your children.

The Importance of Teamwork

Parents certainly will always have the primary responsibility for raising children to love and serve God, but the larger family of the church can play a vital and supportive role. Raising children is a challenge that for disciples needs to extend beyond the immediate family. Parents need all the help they can get! As you serve in the children's ministry, you are there to offer that help. Parents and Kingdom Kids teachers must work together.

A teacher will often see a pattern in a child that the parent has not seen or has taken too lightly. This teacher must love the child enough to share the insight, overcoming the fear of upsetting the parents. On the other hand, the parents must be humble enough to eagerly seek out the teacher's input. It does take a village to raise a child. We must ensure that the village is the kingdom of God and that it is a village where the truth is spoken in love. As a teacher, never underestimate the impact you can have on a child with your love, enthusiasm and conviction. Even more so, don't underestimate the impact that you can have on a parent—who will then have much more time than you do to reinforce what the child needs. An insight you pass on to a humble parent may have a major effect on a child's life.

The Importance of the Grace of God

Let me close with an important thought for parents and teachers. Too often in working with our children (and even with adults), the focus is placed on behavior, to the exclusion of the heart behind the behavior—on *doing* rather than on *being*. This is very dangerous because it can lead to a "performance" or "works" mentality. One of the primary needs in the kingdom of God today is having a better understanding of the grace of God. For example, it feels totally different to me when I do something for God because I love him and want to make him happy, rather than doing something in order to stay out of trouble with him. The "measure up" mentality is a deadly ploy of Satan to get us to rely on ourselves, rather than on God and his mercy. This results in frustration, defeat, deceit and eventually, burnout. God wants the heart, because he knows that when he gets the heart, the actions will follow. Not surprisingly, when questioned about which command-ment is God's most important, Jesus answered,

> "'Love the Lord your God with all your heart and with all your soul and with all your mind.' This is the first and greatest commandment." (Matthew 22:37-38)

Whether the training is taking place in the living room, the kitchen or the children's ministry classroom, it is of primary importance that we all communicate that our faith is about a relationship with a God who loves and believes in us. Our children must learn that we do what we do because we are grateful to be dearly loved children. When our children see this heart in our homes, and have that message rein-forced by thankful teachers in their Kingdom Kids classes, we will all be working together—sending a powerful message to a time that we will not see.

PART 1

Heart-Changing Quiet Times

God Our Father

Gordon Ferguson • Boston, USA

> How great is the love the Father has lavished on us,
> that we should be called children of God! And that
> is what we are!
>
> *1 John 3:1*

God is our Father and those of us in Christ are his specially adopted children—no truth in the Bible is more exciting! The cost of this adoption is the blood of Christ, which should humble us and fill us with a depth of gratitude that becomes our greatest motivation to serve. In fact, the fatherly love of God is what we are to imitate as we serve others in his name. Paul said it this way in Ephesians 5:1-2:

> Be imitators of God, therefore, as dearly loved children and live a life of love, just as Christ loved us and gave himself up for us as a fragrant offering and sacrifice to God.

As we imitate him and live a life of love, we surely must develop his heart for children.

How does the love of God show up in his treatment of us? Keep in mind that this is the kind of love that we are to imitate as disciples and as Kingdom Kids teachers.

Sacrificial Love

From his first contact with man until the present, God has shown himself to be a giver, not a taker. His concern is never what we can do for him, but only what he can do for us. He is absolutely selfless in his relationship to mankind. He gives and gives and gives some more. He is a Servant of servants, which explains how he can keep blessing us when we are unlovely, undeserving and unappreciative.

God does not take our sins against him personally, get his feelings hurt and pull his heart back. He keeps on giving in the hope that his kindness will once again lead us to repentance (Romans 2:4). When Jesus said that the first prerequisite for following him was sacrificial self-denial (Luke 9:23), he was only calling us to do what God has always done. Sacrifice is what God's heart is all about—it is not something that he does, but something that he is. As you serve children, imitate that.

Respectful Love

God shows us respect by treating us as individuals and by expecting us to be the individuals we have been designed to be. He does not expect us to be like everyone else, but to be the best that we can be. The command to "train a child in the way he should go" (Proverbs 22:6) implies the need to understand who each child is and then help him to blossom into the plan of God for his life. Similarly, God does not try to force us into any mold that we were not made for, but patiently develops us into the mold for which we were originally designed.

In essence, God shows us respect in order to help us become respectable. His approach is never to make us *earn* his favor by our performance, but rather, he treats us with love in order to help us grow and mature. As we work with others, we must give them what they need as an impetus to move them in the direction God has planned for them.

Resourceful Love

God uses any and every means available to help us grow into becoming like him. He has a multiplicity of circumstances and people he can call into play for our guidance, and he works everything out for our good. And our ultimate good is "to be conformed to the likeness of his Son" (Romans 8:28-29).

The greatest miracles, in my mind, are not the obvious ones in the Bible, but rather the everyday variety that are produced by God's orchestration of so many behind-the-scenes details. To make the application to us as people helpers, we need to be getting as much (behind-the-scenes) input and help from others as possible. As Proverbs 15:22 puts it, "Plans fail for lack of counsel, but with many advisers they succeed." We must continually be learners if we are to be effective teachers. Don't be lazy and don't be prideful; get help to be your best, and get the help from all available sources.

Positive Love

God's love is *positive* in its expression to us. Positive reinforcement is one obvious demonstration of his kindness and gentleness. He knows exactly how to call us higher by encouraging us. It is easy to think that we help others improve by focusing on their weak points, believing that if they can just eliminate them, then they will really be great. The problem is that the other person's self-esteem takes a beating in the process. God is full of encouragement as he generously expresses his love and commitment to us. With this approach, we can face critiques with confidence.

My wife, Theresa, explains Paul's approach in his letters as a "love sandwich." He begins with positive praise for those in his audience, then delivers his corrections, but finishes with more positive praise and encouragement. Critiques must be balanced with the positives, and most of us need much more praise than correction. Never is this truer than for children, whose self-image is in the process of being formed. Be an encourager and help others believe in what they can become with God's help.

Sensitive Love

God is protective of us, choosing to expose our weaknesses in embarrassing ways only when we are stubborn and prideful. He works gently as he leads us to see ourselves and to resolve to change. Many of us can remember times in our childhood when we were embarrassed by teachers or parents in front of our peers. Such deep hurts are not easily forgotten. Thankfully, God is not that kind of parent. He deals with us gently and sensitively (Isaiah 42:3).

Topics like confidentiality are huge issues in leading and teaching God's children, especially the young ones. Be sensitive with corrections and with keeping confidences. Those whom you lead and teach will not only appreciate it; they will learn to imitate it.

Determined Love

God never gives up trying to mold our characters and hearts into his own image. Gentle he may be, but sentimental he is not! The definition of discipling as "gentle pressure, relentlessly applied" finds its highest application in God's approach with us. He never gives up and he never gives in. His attention to discipling is constant, for he always wants the best for his children. He perseveres with us far beyond what we can imagine. Just think of the story of the runaway son in Luke 15. No matter how long the rebellious son had been gone, the father in the story (representing God) never ceased to gaze at the horizon for any sign of his son's return. When he caught a glimpse of him at a great distance, he literally ran to his son, eagerly accepted his repentance, and then quickly arranged a celebration party of grand proportions. God is determined to save us and determined to help us become the best we can be. How quickly and easily we can be tempted to give up on others. How unlike God we are when we do.

As we look at these amazing qualities of God as our Father, let's determine to imitate them as fully as possible. He wants to express his love to others *through us.* Pray that others will feel his love through your love for them. Love like God loves, and both you and those around you will be filled with inexpressible joy. The love of God is the love of a perfect Parent. Embrace it for yourself, and then share it with others. Let your love for children be the love of God with skin on it, for little ones will understand his love only to the extent that they experience it from those like you.

A Heart to Change

1. *Look back at the six words describing God's love. Which of these areas are strengths and which are weaknesses for you as you teach the children?*
2. *In your interaction with the children in your class, do you focus on their weak points, or do you build their self-esteem through positive praise and encouragement? How will you change?*
3. *Write down ten things you can say to a child to encourage him or her.*
4. *How quickly and easily are you tempted to give up on others—other teachers, the children, the parents?*

Jesus Loved the Children

Joe Farmer • New York City, USA

I didn't like children very much at first. They intimidated me, irritated me and made me feel all kinds of strong emotions, mostly negative. They were hard to predict and harder to control. This may seem typical of a single young man with no children. However, I was not a typical single young man. I was a schoolteacher, and five days a week, six periods a day, they came to me. They came *at* me. They tried my patience and my *soul*. There were moments of triumph and interludes of satisfaction, of course. But these were fleeting compared to the days of quiet (or not so quiet!) frustration that belong to the ineffective teacher. After little more than a year into my first teaching job, I was ready to "move on."

I moved to New York City to pursue my dream of being a professional musician. However, after two years of waiting tables in Manhattan, God had humbled me sufficiently that I was ready to try teaching once again. This time was different. When I walked into P.S. 230 in Brooklyn, New York, I saw children in a completely different light. They challenged me as much as or more than the children in my first teaching job in Cincinnati, Ohio. But this time I saw how much they needed me—how much they needed to be loved by me. And I saw their potential. And oh, how they had potential! One of the girls in that class, an immigrant from Russia named Yuliya, barely spoke English when I first taught her as a fourth grader. She went on to graduate from Stuyvesant High School, widely considered to be one of the finest high schools in the United States.

Jesus' concern for children runs much deeper than just concern for the kind of education they will receive. But the principles remain the same. Jesus saw the incredible potential in children to grow up and do great things for God. And for that reason he sought to protect them from harm brought by sinful men. This is evident in his life and in his teachings. But more than anything, Jesus *loved* the children. He saw the kingdom of heaven in their eyes. He loved them because, just like us, they needed to be loved. And he knew that, in many ways, the future of the kingdom of God rested on how his disciples viewed children. He loved them wholeheartedly and unconditionally. Jesus loves the children, and he wants you to love them too.

Jesus Valued Children

The first time Jesus spoke of children in the New Testament, it was as an object lesson for his selfishly ambitious followers. Jesus saw in a small child the kind of heart that he wanted to see in his disciples. And that is, perhaps, the first lesson we need to learn from Jesus: he *valued* children. He declared the childlike heart to be a prerequisite for entrance into the kingdom. He was so concerned that our sinful natures might not value children as he did, that he made a far-reaching statement about our relationships with them. He said,

> "Whoever welcomes one of these little children in my name welcomes me; and whoever welcomes me does not welcome me but the one who sent me." (Mark 9:37)

We cannot draw close to God and neglect children at the same time. We cannot walk in the footsteps of Jesus and at the same time walk away from children. And we cannot fill our schedules with the "ministry of Jesus," leaving no time for children. Whatever we do to children, we are doing to Jesus. In a world that often had little time or concern for them, children were a priority in Jesus' life, and they must be a priority in our lives.

Jesus Protected Children

There is no getting around Jesus' conviction about protecting children from harm, not just physical harm, but more importantly spiritual harm. Some of the strongest language Jesus ever used is found in his warnings of the consequences of sinning against children. He said,

> "But if anyone causes one of these little ones who believe in me to sin, it would be better for him to have a large millstone hung around his neck and to be drowned in the depths of the sea." (Matthew 18:6)

Jesus stated that, in the end, we would be better off dead than to sin against a child. How do we sin against children? By failing to value them as Jesus did, by failing to protect them as Jesus did, by failing to love them as Jesus did.

When we want to convey to disciples the importance of dealing with their sin decisively and wholeheartedly, we turn to Matthew 18:8-9. Jesus states that,

> "If your hand or your foot causes you to sin cut it off and throw it away. It is better for you to enter life maimed or crippled than to have two hands or two feet and be thrown into eternal fire. And if your eye causes you to sin, gouge it out and throw it away. It is better for you to enter life with one eye than to have two eyes and be thrown into the fire of hell." (Matthew 18:8-9)

Now we know that Jesus is not teaching self-mutilation. You cannot stop a man from lusting by simply gouging out his eyes. There is no physical cure for an unrepentant heart. Jesus is dramatically teaching us the kind of attitude of heart necessary to successfully repent of sin.

But more amazing to me than the content of this verse is its context. In Matthew 18:2 Jesus called a little child to come "stand among them." What follows is Jesus' most extensive teaching on how we are to view children. He concludes by saying, "In the same way your Father in heaven is not willing that any of these little ones should be lost" (Matthew 18:14). The context of "if your hand or your foot causes you to sin cut it off" is in sinning against a child.

Are you aware of how your life is affecting the children around you? Do you realize that they watch you, admire you and imitate you? Do you realize that how you greet children when they come to class can affect how they view God's church? Have you thought about how your interaction with children in their classes can affect their view of God? If you have any attitude that keeps you from fully giving yourself to children—cut it off! The consequences of doing otherwise are unthinkable.

Jesus Desired to Be Close to Children

Like us, sometimes Jesus' disciples were slow learners. In Matthew 18, Jesus taught his disciples how they were to treat children. In

Matthew 19, they demonstrated their need for an immediate review lesson. People were bringing children to Jesus to have him lay his hands on them and pray for them. The disciples, viewing this as an obvious waste of the Master's time, rebuked those who brought the children. How must the children have felt to watch their parents be rebuked by these men of God? Apparently Jesus knew, and he dealt with his disciples decisively (Matthew 19:14).

In Mark's account of this incident, at the end he records that Jesus "took the children in his arms, put his hands on them and blessed them" (Mark 10:16). Jesus wanted them to *feel* his love: to see it in his eyes, to feel it in his touch, to hear it in his voice. Jesus harbored no illusions about what it would take for these children to grow up and become his disciples in the first century. He made the most of this opportunity to impress God's love on the hearts of the children. Jesus desired to be close to children.

Love Never Fails

Mark 9 recounts the healing of a boy with an evil spirit. The father described his son's condition in this way:

> ..."Whenever it seizes him, it throws him to the ground. He foams at the mouth, gnashes his teeth and becomes rigid. I asked your disciples to drive out the spirit, but they could not."
> ..."It has often thrown him into fire or water to kill him. But if you can do anything, take pity on us and help us." (Mark 9:18, 22)

The boy's behavior could only be described as bizarre. And there were many issues that surfaced in this situation: the disciples arguing with the teachers of the law, the faithlessness of both the disciples and the father, the crowd that gathered to watch the drama unfold. But one fact comes through with searing clarity: the boy was in *pain*. And the teachers of the law could not help him. The disciples could not help him. The crowd could not help him. Even his father could not help him. Only when they got him to Jesus was his pain relieved.

There are many powerful lessons for us to learn from this. First, there will be children who come to your classes who will not behave as you would like them to. You may consider their behavior to be inappropriate, unacceptable, even bizarre. Remember that children who "act out" in this way usually do so for one reason: they are in *pain.* The severity of their behavior is simply a measure of the severity of the pain they are in. And unless their condition is physiological in origin, almost always the pain has been inflicted on them by another person. Almost always, they are coping the best way they know how with a situation that is beyond their control. And, like the disciples and the father of the boy, many people have tried to help them and have failed. The only hope these children have is if we can get them to Jesus. And the closest thing they have to Jesus today is *you,* as his disciples.

Every summer, the New York church hosts a weeklong camp for preteens. On the day they arrive for camp, many are not sure they want to be there. When the camp is over, they are sure they are not ready to go home! It is a special time and a special place where children's lives can be touched and transformed by the love of God, the power of the gospel and the devotion of disciples who give up time, money and sleep to show the preteens what the kingdom of God is all about.

But not every child recognizes the opportunity that is before them. Not every child expresses gratitude for the sacrifices made on their behalf. For some, it seems, the more you love them, the more agitated they become. They seem intent on rejecting the love and friendship that is extended to them.

I once asked Sheridan Wright, one of our elders, what he thought of all this. This was his response: "There are some kids who will leave this camp and go off and get involved in all kinds of bad stuff. They may immerse themselves in sin all through high school, college and into adulthood. But someday, they're going to get tired of the sin, the disappointment and the pain. They're going to realize just how lost the world is. And then, they're going to remember. They're going to remember that once, a long time ago, there was a place where they felt totally welcomed, totally safe, totally secure, totally loved. And when they're ready, they'll be back. Because love *never* fails."

In teaching children, there will be times of exhilarating success and times when you feel utterly defeated. My encouragement to you is this: value the children as Jesus did, protect the children as Jesus did, and desire to be close to the children as Jesus did. Jesus loved the children, and love *never* fails.

A Heart to Change

1. *Are children a priority in your life? What do you need to change to welcome them into your life and to value them as Jesus did?*

2. *Do you have Jesus' mind-set to protect children? Is there a sin that you need to repent of that is hindering children?*

3. *Do you desire to be close to children? What do you need to do to make sure the children you teach feel loved by you?*

4. *Are you growing in your ability to love children who challenge your character? Do you believe 1 Corinthians 13:8—that "love never fails"?*

JESUS LOVES THE LITTLE CHILDREN

The Worth of a Child

Joyce Conn • New York City, USA

What is the worth of a child? When given this chapter to write, I spent several days mulling over definitions and explanations. Each one seemed inadequate. How can the value—the worth of a child—be summed up in words?

Defining Value

Often in a courtroom in the United States, a monetary value of thousands and sometimes millions of dollars is placed on a child's life, especially if the child has been harmed or killed through negligence, an accident or malpractice. When news of a tragedy is reported—whether a house burned or a village was raided—most people are touched if children have been harmed. We may hear, "It was horrible for everyone, but especially for the children." Children are increasingly used in advertising campaigns and commercials to influence the public. A laughing baby will always grab our attention. It would seem that most people do value children.

However, take another look. On the streets of most any city, you will find drugs being valued more than a child. In some countries, hundreds of homeless children roam the streets, considered worthless by the authorities. Orphanages are overflowing with children, abandoned or given away by their parents.

In the world, there is a wide discrepancy when it comes to placing value on children. But among disciples, there can be no discrepancy. We must constantly be reminded of how God thinks about our children and how he directs us to view them. Early in Jewish history, God began teaching and giving instructions about children.

These commandments that I give you today are to be upon your hearts. Impress them on your children. Talk about them when you sit at home and when you walk along the road, when you lie down and when you get up. (Deuteronomy 6:6-7)

God commands that we focus on the children. He is telling us to give them all the time they need to be impressed with his care, his wonders and his commands. In this passage God emphasizes quality and quantity time. Focus, focus, focus! The spiritual training of children was vital to the life of the Jewish nation.

Who could have placed a value on the young shepherd boy who later became Israel's king? Or the son Hannah gave to God when he was very young? Most would diminish the worth of a slave's child found floating in a basket among the reeds along the bank of the Nile. Yet God had each of these children marked for a valuable purpose in his plan.

In the same light, our children are vital to the kingdom today. In a few short years God's church will be entrusted to them. We must take stock of our stewardship of these children. Are they getting the best examples, the best teaching, the best training and the best love and care the church has to offer?

The Best Leadership

Several years ago, I was in a leaders' meeting in which we talked about the need for strong, spiritual men to lead the children's ministry. One of the evangelists asked me to be more explicit about the type of leadership I felt the children's ministry needed. I asked him to name the three most spiritually minded men he had in his discipleship group. He did not need time to think about it, but immediately named them. I responded, "We need one of those three to lead the children's ministry in your sector."

This is how we must think about the children. They will become great leaders and great followers in the kingdom if we give them the priority they deserve. If we are holding onto our best leaders for "our ministry" when selecting children's ministry, teen or preteen leaders, we are being shortsighted, and in time, the church will become lukewarm.

Discipling

If we place the proper value on our children, we will see to it that the parents get the discipling they need to raise their children to be disciples. God gives parents the responsibility to teach their children to believe in God with all their hearts and to love and respect him. There are many parents in the church who sincerely want to do this, but they do not know how. Because of their upbringing and because many are young Christians themselves, they need specific direction. Many mistakes are made in parenting, not because of bad hearts, but out of ignorance. Instructing and discipling parents about their children is an essential part of "teaching them to obey everything I have commanded you" (Matthew 28:18-20). If a couple's discipling time is spent primarily talking about friends who are studying the Bible, people being reached out to, and baptisms, with no time devoted to their children, it is another indication of shortsightedness which will weaken the church.

Facilities Planning

"For where your treasure is, there your heart will be also" (Matthew 6:21). How much we value the children is shown in how much we are willing to sacrifice for them. We can no longer justify putting our children in cramped, dark, poorly ventilated rooms because of a money crunch or because that particular auditorium is a great meeting place for the adults. The children cannot be an afterthought in choosing a meeting place for the church. We often show our lack of insight when we sell our houses and move our families across town to enroll them in great schools only to accept makeshift and inadequate spaces in which the children learn the Bible. Not only do we teach and train our children in these places, but we create memories. Go into the classrooms, sit in a small chair, and look around. Is this what we want our children to remember about lessons from the Bible?

Willis Ware, one of the region leaders in New Jersey, is a great example of someone who understands the importance of our children. During a midweek service, he became aware of a class next to his where the children were cramped and could not sing because of the proximity to his men's class. His solution was to move his men's class outside and give the children his room so they could sing and enjoy a great class. This spoke volumes and taught a great lesson, not only to the children about how much he valued them, but also to the men in his class who had to get up and move. This is what I call making an impression that pleases God!

Learning from Children

Another way we overlook the value of our children is to underestimate the impact they could have on the church. When Jesus' disciples wanted to discount the worth of the children by sending them away, Jesus rebuked them. They became his visual aid.

> When Jesus saw this, he was indignant. He said to them, "Let the little children come to me, and do not hinder them, for the kingdom of God belongs to such as these. I tell you the truth, anyone who will not receive the kingdom of God like a little child will never enter it." (Mark 10:14-15)

The church needs the children to help keep it pure. The church needs the children in order to learn humility—to see faith in action. Could it be that Jesus intentionally selected a young boy to share his lunch with the five thousand (John 6:9) when there were adults who also brought food? A young boy would be much more likely to give Jesus the meal without a second thought, believing that Jesus could do anything he wanted with it. A young boy would be happy to be a part of such a wondrous miracle and would never think of taking credit for his contribution. Many of the adults no doubt would not have had such pure motives.

The definition of love in 1 Corinthians 13 is exemplified in a child's pure nature. A child loves freely and will trust again and again, even when his trust has been violated. When a child loves, he keeps no record of wrongs. He forgives over and over. Is a child patient? Maybe not when it comes to an ice cream cone or a swimming party. But I have seen a young boy sit on the front steps with his glove and ball waiting all day for his father who promised to show up but never did. A child has great endurance when it comes to those he loves. We need to watch and learn.

The children need to know they are an important part of the kingdom. When they are included, whether it be a family play day or a Bring Your Neighbor Day, the rewards are great. The children bring visitors—who would say no to a child? Children on stage singing songs or reciting scriptures brings joy to the worship service. "Let the children come to me"; don't exclude them. They are an invaluable treasure.

It has been said, and rightfully so, that the children's ministry disciples the church. Any teacher in the children's classes will honestly say that he learned more from teaching the children than the children learned from him. The children's ministry helps keep the church pure. Family problems often come to a leader's attention through the children's ministry. Following up with a family when a child is often absent from class, acts out in class or is withdrawn is very important. Children, in their innocence, unknowingly say things in class that indicate when a family needs help.

A spiritual heart disease (like pride) can be reversed when a disciple is asked to teach a class. There is no recognition, no pat on the back, no impressive stats and no applause.

We need the children to help us keep God's commands simple and clear—and to remind us of what a pure heart looks like. We need the children to help us see our mistakes, to help us examine where we are going and to help us maintain a vision for the future. What is the worth of a child to his parents, to the church, to God? Simply put, a child is *priceless.*

A Heart to Change

1. *God has a plan for each child in your class. What is your vision for them individually and collectively? What is your vision for yourself as you teach them?*

2. *If you are in a decision-making role, do you deliberately show foresight by placing your most spiritually minded and mature disciples in leadership roles with the children? Do you make what is best for the children's ministry a key factor as you select a facility in which to meet? Even if you do not make these decisions, do you have the conviction to speak up when you feel as if these needs are being neglected? How will you change?*

3. *If you disciple couples who have children, do you frequently give specific direction to them during your discipleship times together to help them disciple their children?*
4. *What can you learn from the children in your class about being purer in heart yourself?*

BRING YOUR BIBLE AND COME

Inspiring Love for God and His Word

Ron & Linda Brumley • Seattle, USA

Children love the fun, the exciting, the interactive. They love people who love them, take them seriously, listen to them, make them laugh and comfort them when they're sad. I (Ron) observed hundreds of children in my thirty-year career as an elementary school teacher and principal. I watched the magic of children bonding with their teachers as if each were the only child in the class. I watched the magic of teachers capturing the attention of and leading twenty-five to thirty-five children at a time toward learning and growth. In fact the younger the child, the greater the eagerness and trust. This is surely one of the reasons why Jesus said that we must become like little children in order to enter the kingdom (Matthew 18:3). It is likewise the reason why we must hold as a sacred trust the ability to influence this pure-hearted and receptive audience to love God and his word.

Somebody They Love, Loves God

Children love to be loved—and to love in return. They respond dramatically to being enjoyed and delighted in. Children who enter a classroom in which the teachers are genuinely thrilled to see them are infinitely more likely to be happy to be there and responsive to what those teachers have to say. Children are prone to love what the object of their affection loves. For example, as a child, I (Linda) thought rain was wonderful simply because my mother loved rain. To this day, while others complain about gray skies and drizzle, I delight in it. How did this happen? I loved my mom, and I thought she was basically right about everything. If she said something was good, I trusted her—and I imitated her responses.

Do you remember the seemingly insignificant events from your childhood that had a lasting impact on your life? Never underestimate the way God will use one hour or one conversation in your life. This alone should provide every teacher with the motivation to make every class session vibrant. Having an eternal impact needs to be what we dream about, pray about and prepare for every week during the months when we serve in the children's ministry.

How does a teacher, who has only a few hours each week with a child, make that child feel loved? How does a teacher have lasting impact on a child who is only in class sporadically or perhaps only on one occasion? Smiles, hugs, energy, focus and met needs are a few factors. For the children who are in class week after week, much of their retention depends on the love they experience. However, for the children who only come to service once, much of what they retain depends on the fun and excitement of the class. Of course, even the fun and excitement are the result of a teacher who prepares and teaches out of love for God, love for his word and love for the children.

The One Who Loves Them Gave Us the Bible

The profound, inconceivable love of the Creator is compelling. God, who decided to put children on earth, wants to communicate with them. And as teachers, we have the privilege of acquainting them with that love before they can even read about it for themselves. God determined the times and places where they should live—*and that they would have opportunity to be in your classroom*—so that they would perhaps reach out and find out about his love and his plan for their lives (Acts 17:26-27). What a privilege it is to play a role in this! We as teachers do not just offer them truth, although this is profound—we offer them God's love. No child is too young to begin understanding the love of God (2 Timothy 3:15). When we help children to understand God's love for them, we give them reason to love him back (1 John 4:19), and a relationship is begun.

Here are some practical ways to teach this concept. When the children sing in your class, tell them that singing was God's idea and that he loves to hear them sing. When you help them memorize scriptures, have your own sense of wonder that you are helping them to hide God's word in their hearts (Psalm 119:11) and that it will produce fruit there (Isaiah 55:10-11). When you do crafts with them, chat during the process about the tie-in to the lesson, and emphasize the excitement of the Bible story. Let them know how amazing it is that God works so hard to touch us with his love—creating us, putting us in families, working through different men through thousands of years to write the Bible, sending his own Son to live out an example for us and to finally die for us—just so we could know him and live with him forever.

Every story in the Bible has clues to God's nature and reveals evidence of his love. Approach every lesson with the desire to show your class the nature of God. You can't give what you don't have, so kindle the flame of your own love for God and his word. Let it burn brightly as you teach. The children will see your love for God in your enthusiasm, your animation and your prepared materials and visuals. Ultimately, it is your own love for God and the Bible that will make your teaching experience a joy for you and a benefit to your students.

A Heart to Change

1. *Do you feel excitement or dread about serving in the children's ministry? Why?*
2. *What can you change so that the children will more clearly see your love for God and them through your enthusiasm, animation, prepared materials and visuals?*
3. *Do you see the Word as the answer to the challenges children are facing in today's world? How can you make a difference?*
4. *How can you more effectively communicate your love for God—and love and respect for his word—to the children in your classroom?*

MY GOD IS SO GREAT

Learning from Children

Debbie Wright • New York City, USA

Can you imagine Elijah's surprise? Here he is, having a terrible day (1 Kings 19:1-5). After a great victory at Mt. Carmel against the prophets of Baal, Jezebel threatens Elijah's life, and he falls apart and runs away. He is totally discouraged and in desperate need of having his faith revived. So, God has him stand on a mountain so that he can see him pass by. Elijah is expecting a great manifestation of the power of God which will strengthen his faith. A mighty wind comes, but God is not there. An earthquake shakes the mountain, but God is not there. Next a fire appears, but again, God is not there. Finally, God appears—but in a gentle whisper (1 Kings 19: 11-13). This was not what Elijah expected, but it was what he needed.

God is God and he will act in any manner he chooses, because he is sovereign over all. This was all that Elijah needed to know. When threatened by Jezebel, instead of panicking, God had expected him to listen to him, just as he expects the same of us today.

In Matthew 18:1-4, Jesus says that unless we change and become like little children, we will never enter the kingdom of heaven. The children's ministry affords an incredible opportunity to practice the truth of this scripture. Sometimes we get so busy teaching that we don't step back and study the children to see the lessons God has made available for us personally. Like Elijah, we just have to listen for his "gentle whisper" coming through these little lives.

Childlike Humility

Perhaps the most obvious lesson we can learn from children is humility. Children, naturally, from a very young age, humbly ask question after question about all kinds of things. "Why is the sky blue?" "Why is there air?" "Do pets go to heaven?" Children attack life with gusto, wanting to know everything about everything. They know that they are the ones who don't know. They have no problem with not knowing; they just want to find out. They are not afraid to ask because they have nothing to lose.

How about us? As adults, do we have this same thirst for knowledge about God and his will for us? Perhaps we have stopped seeking and become more robotic in our walk with God. Pride wants us to protect our lack of knowledge by creating an *appearance* of knowledge. Humility has nothing to protect and is eager to learn. Pride is opposed by God, and the prideful person remains ignorant. Humility is exalted, thus allowing us to change and grow into the likeness of Christ.

Another aspect of a child's humility is trust. Children assume that their parents will protect them. They assume that their parents will provide for them. It doesn't matter to them how bad a situation may be; they feel that if they can just be with their parents, then everything will be all right.

When we were teaching our children to swim, we would have them stand on the side of the pool while we would back up a considerable distance in the pool, and then tell them to jump to us. They would look at the water and then at us, but when they jumped, they would focus on us the entire time, never looking at the water. They trusted *us* more than they feared the water. This is how God wants all of us to be with him. As adults we somehow "mature" into not trusting. It is easier for us to let our fear of the obstacle or challenge or hardship be our focus, and as a consequence, our faith and our lives suffer defeat. We need to change and become like children, trusting God implicitly.

Childlike Resilience

Another quality in children worth imitating is their resilience. It is amazing how children can experience many hurtful things and have a period of being upset and crying, but then they can simply focus on something else and move on. Sometimes they don't even remember the "devastation" they suffered just a few hours earlier.

However, as adults we grow up and acquire a sense of entitlement, which hinders our resilience. We feel that we are entitled to certain things: life has to go our way, people should be fair, and bad things should not happen to us. And when life is not like this, we brood and give ourselves over to a bitter spirit. In contrast, children get over it when things don't go their way because they know that there is more to life than just one dream. There are other dreams that can be taken hold of, and they move on to explore these possibilities. Is it any wonder Jesus said to change and become like little children?

Childlike Forgiveness

One other lesson we can learn from children is one that is desperately needed today: forgiveness. Notice how children handle conflict. They get angry, say mean things, hurt each others' feelings, shed tears and mope—for a little while. Then they say they are sorry and begin playing as if nothing ever happened. Children put a high value on friendship. They do not want anything to interfere with this. Even when they have been hurt, they want things to be resolved quickly so that they can be friends again. This is why they are eager to accept an apology, put the incident behind them and go play again.

Children also are sensitive to the times when they have needed forgiveness and how bad a person feels until they are forgiven, so they don't want to "rub it in." Retribution is an adult concept, for the most part. We want the offender to experience at least as much hurt as the offended. Therefore, forgiveness seems to come slowly and grudgingly. Think of how much more pleasant life is when we act like children and care more about our relationships than our rights, enjoying the freedom to forgive.

Yes, Elijah sure was surprised on that mountain. Yet that will be nothing compared to the joyful surprise we will continue to experience as God teaches us through the children. God has a tendency to turn things upside down, and this happens in the Kingdom Kids classroom: he expects the teachers to become the students. We who teach will experience a special gratitude on the Day of Judgment. While we will be grateful for the fact that God used us to make a difference and help save the souls of our students, we will also be grateful that God saved our souls because we opened our hearts and listened to his gentle whisper in the lives of the ones we taught.

A Heart to Change

1. *Cite a specific example of a situation in which a child has taught you a lesson.*
2. *What other attributes (not discussed in this chapter) do children have that challenge adults?*
3. *What adult disciples do you know who best exemplify the hearts of children? What do you see in their lives?*
4. *How can you best prepare yourself to be taught by the children that you will be teaching?*

Jesus' Heart for Service

Larry Wood • Boston, USA

> Jesus said to them, "The kings of the Gentiles lord it over them; and those who exercise authority over them call themselves Benefactors. But you are not to be like that. Instead, the greatest among you should be like the youngest, and the one who rules like the one who serves. For who is greater, the one who is at the table or the one who serves? Is it not the one who is at the table? But I am among you as one who serves.
>
> *Luke 22:25-27*

Jesus' role as a servant is a very familiar concept to most of us who have been around the kingdom for even a short time. Verses jump quickly to mind and we remember great sermons during which we were challenged to be servants like Jesus. Many of you reading this are like me and have even taught this very concept to your friends and even your children. The challenge we all face is being able to say with Paul that what we teach agrees with the way we live (1 Corinthians 4:17).

Walking the Talk

We are guilty of the greatest hypocrisy when we are familiar with scriptures about serving, encouraging, discipling—and many more—but do not live them out. Some of us can speak at great length of what we have seen, heard and even done in our time. We have taught those accounts in the Gospels when the disciples argued about which of them was the greatest. Some of us may even have washed others' feet in an effort to be like Jesus. But these are distant memories. We have read Paul's call to imitate Jesus in our attitudes and hearts, but familiarity and life's circumstances have led us to a place where serving is a good idea, but not one we embrace and engage with our hearts. We have exhausted our energies on building our lives, and there is no time left to serve.

After three years of laboring and giving, Jesus, facing an imminent cross, had to again settle a dispute among the twelve about who was the greatest. Any of us would be quite sympathetic had Jesus said, "Are you still so dull?" A rebuke, or perhaps another parable, would have seemed appropriate. Instead, Jesus simply said, "I am among you as one who serves." And then he took up a towel to lower himself to the humble role of washing feet.

In my early years I had no limit of energy and zeal for serving—whatever the need, wherever it was, whenever. Go anywhere; do anything; give up everything! This was my vision. Now, some twenty years later, I find that an excuse or an exception often follows "anywhere." "Do anything" is interpreted through a long to-do list that must be accomplished before anything else is possible. And "give up everything" has become a history lesson of what I have given up in the past as a justification for what I am not able to give up now.

My experience is that I am not all that different from many disciples around me. I must struggle to have the heart of a servant. I am challenged to have serving be the context of my life.

Heart Surgery

Children's ministry often exposes my heart. It calls me back to Jesus, who, as his time on earth was coming to an end, summed up his life with one sentence: "I am among you as one who serves." Had he not served enough? Was he not Lord, and could he not look at James or Peter and delegate serving to them? Would the disciples not have benefited even more from a lesson about serving—with an exercise of pairing off to wash each other's feet? The Scriptures are quite emphatic: No! Jesus encapsulated his life in a single sentence and then gave them an example they would never forget.

What is the application here for me? What is the application for you? First, when Jesus wanted to identify who he was at the very heart, he stated, "I am among you as one who serves." That is my identity—who I am. I am a disciple. I am a businessman. I am a father. I am a leader. But because I follow Jesus, I am above all a servant. Jesus, as he went to the cross, wanted his most intimate group of friends to see him as a servant. After teaching them yet again, he gave a vivid visual reinforcement. He took up the weapon of a servant—a towel—and washed their dirty feet. All discussion of greatness or role was silenced by an event none of them ever could have predicted. Jesus saw the need. He knew the situation. He knew who he was. So he served. Of all the "I am" statements in the Gospels, this one stands out as one these men had perhaps the greatest difficulty grasping.

Are we that much different? We may scoff at their dullness. But when we see needs and know the situation in the children's ministry, how do we respond? Do we offer the "Don't You Know Who I Am" speech? Maybe it is the "I Have a More Important Role to Fulfill" conversation? Some see themselves as being above this type of service. Many point out that they have served recently—and is there not someone else available who could do it? Jesus could have offered any one of these as reasons for why the time was not right for him to serve, but Jesus considered his role unequivocally to be that of a servant. I am confident that any thought of having "done enough" did not even cross his mind. You cannot read the Scriptures and miss the fact that though Jesus was the King of Kings, he identified himself as a servant—with no qualifications or limits.

Unlimited Willingness

If you are reading this, you have likely just been asked to serve as a teacher. Let me call you to look one more time at Jesus' heart to serve. Two characteristics of Jesus' service stand out for those serving in the children's ministry. First, Jesus had no limit to his willingness to serve. As a children's ministry leader I am sometimes given a list of busy-ness and life's challenges to explain why it's not a good time for serving the children. Sure, there can be legitimate reasons, but we all need to remember that taking up a towel was likely not on Jesus' to-do list just before going to the cross. There was still much that needed to be done. He could easily have justified an "I Need a Break" talk, considering what he had been doing and what he was facing. But the need of the moment was for someone to serve.

No qualifiers. No excuses. No limits. Just a willing heart to take up a towel and meet the need.

Unsung Heroes

A second way that our hearts are exposed in children's ministry is that this type of service may not offer immediate results or recognition. Most children are not poised at the edge of the baptistery about to make their decision for Christ. They require attention and focus and labor that may only result in them taking away with them a great memory from the class that day. We are in an age in which many want instant results. Children's ministry often does not offer immediate rewards. Combine this with a lack of recognition, and we find that it is a struggle for some to get motivated to teach. For some, children's ministry is one more thing to do on an already overextended list.

When Jesus washed the disciples' feet, it was not a glorious deed. It was not one that this brought great recognition, fame or honor. It was purely an act of service. But because Jesus was a servant to his core, I am confident that this single act was as fulfilling to him as any of the dramatic miracles he performed. Jesus did not need recognition. In fact, he preferred anonymity in his serving.

What moved Jesus was the need he saw and his servant's heart, which brought him to earth. As you answer the request to serve, can you find motivation and fulfillment in meeting a need whether or not anyone but God sees your effort? Can you offer your service, preferring anonymity, like Jesus?

Servants Serve

Great poets write because they are poets. Great painters paint because they are painters. Great servants serve because they are servants. If you were to capture in one word who Jesus was, you might say "Savior." You might confess him as Lord. You might even speak at great length about Jesus being the Son of God. But when Jesus wanted to capsulize his life in a single sentence—his role, his talent, his heart, his very identity—he simply stated: "I am among you as one who serves." As you enter your time of being with the children, hear Jesus calling you to be like him, and see yourself as a servant.

A Heart to Change

1. Can you personally find motivation and fulfillment in meeting a need even if no one but God sees your effort? Can you offer your service in anonymity like Jesus did?
2. In your ministry group, family, children's class or in the church, what would you say identifies who you are?
3. What do you see as being the unmet needs in the children's ministry in your region? What solutions and ways to help and serve can you offer?
4. Who are some of the tireless servants in children's ministry whom you know? How can you best imitate their faith, their convictions and their hearts? Will you take a moment to express your gratitude to them for their example?

OH, BE CAREFUL

Influencing Children

Vicki Jacoby • Washington, D.C., USA

It amazes me, after an hour and a half at a movie theater with my three children, how much they have heard and retained—and how they have even memorized lines. The accents, the attitudes and the actions of the characters on-screen are so influential. Children are receptive, teachable, moldable—so eager to learn.

We have that same opportunity to influence children as we give them our hearts, our attention and our energy. They are waiting to be influenced, daring us to leave an impression on them. And the fact is that if we do not determine to have that impact, the world certainly will. Phenomenally strong pressure is placed on our children to conform to the pattern of this world (Romans 12:1-2).

Combating the World

The commercialization around us affects our children, especially in the First World. We have only just recovered from the Beanie Baby craze to walk into Pokémon fever. As parents, we stare in amazement as yet another product assaults our children—and they fall for it, completely under the spell. And so much of what we allow our children to view, to experience and to be exposed to tears at their very souls. Are money and glamour really more important than people? Is Hollywood "love" the real thing and married (Biblical) love something inferior? Are our principles as disciples fundamentally no different from the values of the world? We must never underestimate the influence of the world.

Of course some influences are not necessarily negative. Think about why we choose to have children in the first place. We want to create someone to love, someone who belongs to us. We want to influence them, to impart wisdom to them. God created man for this reason: that we perhaps might reach out for him, although he is not far from us (Acts 17:24-27).

Positive Influences

God wants to influence us and our children through his word and a relationship with him. We know that, with the Bible, we can influence mankind and see this world won for Jesus Christ in our generation. These are healthy influences, assuming the children see us modeling these principles in our lives. (They see right through us when we are being hypocritical!) The question is, *In the whirlwind of influences swirling around our children's heads and hearts, which influences will prevail?*

In children's ministry it's our turn to influence children, to help them find God, though he is not far from them. They need a relationship with us in order to understand a relationship with God. It would be nice if the children would figure out the truth apart from adult influence, but this is not realistic. We will be either their inspiration or their excuse.

A children's ministry worker who walks with God is not only an upward call, but a flesh and blood example of what it means to enjoy the Christian life. Children look at us, longing for the joy and peace that come from a wholehearted walk with the Lord. What do the children see in you?

Of course, the prime character shapers of children are always parents. The church can never take the place of the parents in bringing up children in a spiritual way, nor was it ever intended to. If it was, the Bible would most likely contain specific instruction on how to build a children's ministry—but it does not. However, we do find many passages directed to parents, such as Deuteronomy 6:1-9 and Ephesians 6:1-4. Yet teachers in the children's ministry also occupy a vital niche in the spiritual upbringing of our precious children.

Lasting Impact

Our family has moved to different countries a number of times (England, Australia, Sweden, the United States), and our three children have been influenced by the children's ministry and teachers in each place. I am very grateful for the inspiring children's ministry in London. My husband and I lived and worked in London for many years, the last time being late 1994 to early 1996. Our children, James, Emma and Lily, thoroughly enjoyed the superb children's ministry overseen by the London elders. Their approach to placing dedicated teachers in the children's ministry shows their determination to influence the children who visit their classes. Now, four years later, after returning to the United States, our children still have relationships with their teachers back in London.

One of those teachers, Rachel, remembers Emma's birthday. They spend time together whenever we visit the London church, and Emma (now nine years old) sleeps over at Rachel's home. Another teacher, Giovanni, came over to play chess with James, then seven. Now eleven, James has learned not only chess from Gio, but also a love for Jesus Christ that has stayed with him. And Lily was two-and-a-half when we moved to the United States. She would often say how much she missed London and her children's ministry teachers. Now six, she is going to be a flower girl in her current children's ministry teacher's wedding.

When our region recently moved from two curriculum classes each week to one due to space limitations and teacher ratio requirements, our children were disappointed: "We miss the old way. When can we have regular Wednesday church again?" As far as they are concerned, the more church, the better.

Does this sound unusual? It is not unusual when there is a friendship, a relationship, between teacher and student. Influence comes naturally through relationships. Children know whether you are giving them your heart; they know whether you have time for them. They can sense your love for God through your patience and careful instruction. A dedicated, wholehearted children's ministry worker has a chance to affect a child for eternity.

A Sober Estimate

If you have not been giving your whole heart, consider the thoughts above as you recommit yourself to the children. If you have been giving one hundred percent, but perhaps have not felt supported by parents and leaders, stick to your convictions. It is not the approval of this generation we live for, nor even of the next. Servants of Christ have but one Master (Galatians 1:10, Colossians 3:23-24, Ephesians 6:9).

A Heart to Change

1. *Make a list of five worldly influences that shape our children. What is your reaction to these influences?*
2. *Do you see the relationship between you and your students as being one that can lead to long-term friendships?*
3. *To what in your own life have you ever given one hundred percent? What do you need to change in your life now in order to serve the children wholeheartedly?*

BUILDING UP THE KINGDOM

Building a Great Children's Ministry

Larry & Lea Wood • Boston, USA

What we have heard and known,
   what our fathers have told us.
We will not hide them from their children;
   we will tell the next generation
the praiseworthy deeds of the Lord,
   his power, and the wonders he has done.
He decreed statutes for Jacob
   and established the law in Israel,
which he commanded our forefathers
   to teach their children,
so the next generation would know them,
   even the children yet to be born,
   and they in turn would tell their children.
Then they would put their trust in God
   and would not forget his deeds
   but would keep his commands.

Psalm 78:3-7

Our movement's chief purpose is to reach the world with the message of Jesus. Much focused thought and prayer have gone into reaching this goal. To the credit of our leaders and their efforts, the plan is working, as many new souls are being won every day throughout the world. Unfortunately, this is not as true with our children. Many of our efforts have been more about baby-sitting than building, more keeping them busy than encouraging their faith, and more occupying their attention than really meeting their needs.

Our conviction is that unless we have a plan to reach our children and to build their faith, the future existence of God's movement—and its purpose—will be severely endangered. We will find ourselves scrambling to catch up with the world that has spent many years shipwrecking our children's faith through humanistic teaching and the powerful use of the media. One thing that has become ever so certain to us in our time as parents and children's ministry leaders is this: Satan has a plan for our children!

When you consider your role in God's kingdom, realize the importance of your time working with the children. Whether planning classes, training teachers or discipling parents, you can be sure that this ministry is integral to laying the foundation that will carry the movement of God to children yet to be born.

The Lesson of Israel

As we measure all of our ministries by the number of generations of faithful disciples, so we must take stock of our children's ministry. We must understand that the children who are in the children's ministry are future leaders who will carry God's message—and God's movement—to the next generation. The daunting nature of this task is apparent when you consider that many great men of the Bible failed to build faith in their children

The history of Israel is filled with the failure of the nation to fulfill David's psalm. It was the *rare* case when one generation passed its righteousness to the next one. Noah, Samuel and David are a few great men of the Bible whose children did not walk in their ways. We must have this as one of our deepest convictions: Unless we build dynamic, powerful children's ministries, our movement will not enjoy long-term success.

The 'Big Picture'

Fix these words of mine in your hearts and minds; tie them as symbols on your hands and bind them on your foreheads. Teach them to your children, talking about them when you sit at home and when you walk along the road, when you lie down and when you get up. Write them on the doorframes of your houses and on your gates, so that your days and the days of your children may be many in the land that the Lord swore to give your forefathers, as many as the days that the heavens are above the earth. (Deuteronomy 11:18-21)

Before any teachers will prepare a quality class that leaves a child eager for more, they must first get the "big picture" of what the ultimate purpose of the children's ministry is: to build a child's faith in God. Teachers must understand that they are working with parents to develop a child's faith and encourage him or her to love God from the heart. They must prepare and teach classes that make God real to them. Moses parting the Red Sea. David slaying Goliath. Daniel spending the night with lions. Jesus resurrected from the dead. Epoch Bible stories come alive as children hear about the faith and courage of great men and women of God. The history of God must be written on the hearts and minds of our children.

Unfortunately, for too many of our children, a sobering reality is that their weekly classes are the most focused spiritual time they experience. If our classes are weak, poorly planned or uninspired, they give children the wrong impression of God. As a teacher, you can never underestimate how one class can influence a child's thinking about God. A crucial fact that teachers must appreciate is that God has entrusted these few vulnerable souls to them to teach and train—if only for a few hours each week.

Before focusing on the nuts and bolts of teaching, you must first focus on your heart. A teacher who has a heart for children will find out what it takes to prepare a great class—or be humble enough to get help in making his or her class excellent. Teachers whose hearts are not with the children will at best do mediocre classes, regardless of how many practical suggestions are made to help them. As is always the case, the heart is the foremost issue. You must set your heart to give your all to the children or relegate these children to a lukewarm experience.

Building a Ministry

A children's ministry is only as good as the teachers staffing the classes. Teachers must strive to imitate Jesus as they work with children. You are playing a meaningful and vital role in God's kingdom.

When you appreciate this, you will develop the skills to be a great teacher and to "stay on top of your ministry."

According to James 3:1, those who teach will be judged more strictly. For an allotted time each week, God, along with the leaders and parents, has entrusted the children to your care. Your leaders feel *you* have something to give to the children. You must decide to take this seriously and understand the privilege it is to be with the kingdom's children.

Decide to do whatever it takes to make classes great. Be thoughtful and prepared. Your children's class cannot be an afterthought of your weekly priorities. It must be something you pray about and give considerable time to preparing. No amount of energy and enthusiasm will make up for a poorly prepared, disorganized class. Recognize that teaching children demands creativity, imagination and resourcefulness. If these are weaknesses in your character, you will have the opportunity to change in great ways. If these are talents of yours, you will be able to use them in ways you never thought possible.

In the end, you will find that teaching children is one of the most rewarding experiences in the kingdom of God. Most disciples we know who have invested their lives in blessing children through teaching in the children's ministry have come away from the experience changed. They are better disciples for having given themselves to God's children. Remember: You are not a baby-sitter—build your ministry!

A Heart to Change

1. *How has this chapter changed your view of the "big picture"? How does this change affect how you view your role as a teacher?*
2. *If you are currently teaching, how much time did you put into preparation for the class last week? If you're not teaching yet, will you think of a weekly time that you will set aside for preparation?*
3. *Who will you ask for advice in teaching your age group? Do you know who the "expert teachers" are in your ministry? Remember that humility is key.*

TAKE THE LORD WITH YOU

Walking with God

Jayne Ricker • San Diego, USA

Our God is an amazing God! As I sat by the Pacific Ocean on a brilliant, sunny morning to gather my thoughts for this chapter, I stopped and considered God's wonders (Job 37:14). I could smell the ocean air and feel the cool breeze—that God stirs up, of course—and I marveled at the endless sea, which is his (Psalm 95:5). My eyes wandered up to the sky he spread out (Job 37:18). I remembered what his word said about his great love for me—so great that it is higher than the heavens—and that his faithfulness reaches to the skies (Psalm 108:4). I thought about the countless stars in the sky and the measureless sand on the seashore (Jeremiah 33:22). I was amazed. I looked to my right to see his mighty mountains, which he compares to his righteousness (Psalm 36:6). I thought, "My ears had heard of you but now my eyes have seen you" (Job 42:5).

When my heart is focused on how big and wonderful my God really is, it is very easy for me to feel close to him. The times when I am obeying his word, believing in his promises and marveling at his creation, are the most incredible times of my life. To walk with him throughout my day knowing, "Whom have I in heaven but you? And earth has nothing I desire besides you" (Psalm 73:25) is a precious gift from God indeed. We are ready to teach our children when we come to them from our walk with God.

Walking Through the Valley

There have been, however, those times when I have not walked closely with God and so have felt lonely on my spiritual journey. I have known times when I seemed to be barely hanging on to the tip of God's finger, instead of feeling his arms wrapped tightly around me. Those were hard times, and one of them was not too long ago. My husband, Bob, a great disciple of Jesus for more than sixteen years, was diagnosed with melanoma (a malignant, third-stage skin cancer) at the age of thirty-seven. It is a lethal cancer. Every diagnosis we received was worse than the previous one—my husband was going to die. God revealed to me during that time that my walk with him was quite shallow.

> Even though I walk
>   through the valley of the shadow of death,
> I will fear no evil,
>   for you are with me;
> your rod and your staff,
>   they comfort me. (Psalm 23:4)

I, however, was filled with fear. I felt as though God had deserted me forever. I had absolutely no comfort in my heart. As my husband continued to worsen physically, although always growing spiritually, I realized that I had better draw much closer to God. I had to walk with God like never before if I was going to pass this faith test.

It finally struck me, after much discipling, prayer and fasting, that I could only depend on God. His promises would pull me through. He is a good God and his plans are perfect. Needless to say, when I realized this and made the decision to trust God, there was an amazing transformation in my heart and in my life. I depended on scriptures such as Philippians 1:21-23 and John 14:1-2. When I started walking closely with God, Romans 8:35-38 gave me enormous comfort. I began living out 1 Corinthians 15:58:

> Therefore, my dear brothers, stand firm. Let nothing move you. Always give yourselves fully to the work of the Lord, because you know that your labor in the Lord is not in vain.

Knowing that God loved me enabled me to stand firm despite my circumstances.

The disciples closest to me were amazed at the changes in my life. My nondisciple friends were astonished. My husband went to meet our God on December 5, 1997, and I could preach with confidence that Jesus was right in saying:

"I am the resurrection and the life. He who believes in me will live, even though he dies; and whoever lives and believes in me will never die." (John 11:25-26)

Not only did I feel my hand in God's hand, but I felt as though his arms were wrapped around me and would never let me go. I finally had peace that surpassed all understanding. From that time on, I never missed a beat in life and gave myself fully to the work of the Lord.

The Radiance Factor

It is obvious in disciples' lives when they are walking with God. Abraham was walking closely with God when he went up the mountain to sacrifice his one and only son—a son for whom he had waited for one hundred years. He knew that God had the plan and that his plan was perfect. How about you? Is it obvious to the children you teach in the children's ministry that you have a great walk with God? What are you *really* teaching the children in your children's ministry class? What does your face say when you have had a hard Sunday morning? Are you joyful and thankful *always,* or does it depend on your circumstances? (1 Thessalonians 5:16-18). Do you let go of God's hand when things do not go your way? How do you react when hard times unexpectedly invite themselves into your life—and you have absolutely no say in the matter?

When your time comes to walk through a dark valley (and it will come, if it hasn't already), will you stay close to God and fear no evil? How about right now? Do you feel like God is with you more than ever? Do you have comfort that his promises will sustain you? Do you rejoice in your sufferings (Romans 5:3-4) because they produce heavenly qualities in your heart? Do your daily times with God enable you to become more like Jesus? Are you obtaining joy in your life solely on the basis of your relationship with God? If you can say a resounding, "Yes!"—then you are having a great walk with God. If your answer is not so clearly "Yes," but you eagerly desire to get to that point, you, too, are walking with God, and he will bless you.

Live the Lessons

We read in John 5:39-40 that the Pharisees diligently studied the Scriptures—but never connected with Jesus. This is a scary thought.

What does God see in your life and heart? Does he see a Pharisee or someone who has a desperate need for him? Off and on for many years as a disciple, I would revert to pharisaical ways, like being happy in church but complaining about the little things at home. I would serve my leaders, but I would not serve my family with a grateful heart. I would direct disciples to share their faith, but I did not have a heart that loved the lost. I would have sin in my heart, but I would not confess it. It is an ugly and lonely place to be when you are in God's glorious kingdom and your ways are those of a Pharisee.

Jesus was very direct with the Pharisees of his time, and he is very direct with us today. Jesus says many times in Matthew 23, "Woe to you, teachers of the law and Pharisees." We can look good on the outside (Matthew 23:25-28), but our insides can be full of sin. Imagine teaching our children using the great Kingdom Kids Curriculum, making excellent crafts and learning memory scriptures, but totally leaving God out of the picture. We simply would not convert their hearts to Jesus. There is no way to teach children how to walk closely with God if we are not walking closely with God ourselves. Jesus knew that the Pharisees did not have the love of God in their hearts (John 5:42), and he was heartbroken about it (Matthew 23:37). If we are not walking closely with God *daily,* we could very likely "shut the kingdom of heaven in [our children's] faces" (Matthew 23:13) and make our children sons of hell (Matthew 23:15) because of the lack of love in our hearts toward God. Are we going to be like those teachers of the law and Pharisees? Or will we be teachers with hearts for God who can transfer our hearts to our children so that they will never have to walk alone in their lives?

Fight the Enemy

It is vitally important to remember that Satan wants you to walk only with him and not with God. Revelation 12:17 states that he is enraged at the woman and wars against the rest of her offspring, "those who obey God's commandments and hold to the testimony of Jesus." The offspring Satan is after includes every child sitting in your midweek and Sunday classes. Satan wants to "take them out." He may very well aim to do that by taking us out.

He loves it when we do not meditate on the wonders of God every morning. He loves it when we do not see our daily need for God. He loves it when are not totally fixated on God throughout the day and growing in this every day. Walking with God is a lifelong challenge and a daily decision. It must change your life and your relationships.

May it be said of all of us that we walked with God and then we were no more, because God took us away (Genesis 5:24). If you are walking closely with God, you will have a joy and a peace that surpasses understanding. You will rely on his promises and stand firm through the trials and tests. You will transfer your heart. You will teach the children in your class to love and walk with God.

A Heart to Change

1. *How do you handle the trials in your life? Which scriptures could you memorize to help you stand firm and give yourself fully to the work of the Lord during the hard times?*
2. *Do those closest to you see your walk with God as worthy of imitation?*
3. *Is your walk with God one that you would eagerly transfer and teach to both the children and the other teachers in your class? What will you decide to change today to ensure that your walk with God continues to grow?*

DEEP DOWN IN MY HEART

Attitude of Excellence

Amby Murphy • Boston, USA

And now I will show you the most excellent way.
1 Corinthians 12:31

Jesus loved the little children. He loved grown-up sinners. He was moved by a mother's love (Luke 7:11-15), grieved by a father's loss (Luke 8:49-50) and was touched by the untouchable leper's plea for mercy (Mark 1:40-42). He loved his father's house and refused to see it reduced to a den of robbers (Mark 11:15-17). Whatever the circumstances, Jesus did everything well (Mark 7:37). In every situation he showed love because he understood that, in fact, love is the most excellent way.

As we serve and teach our children, we will have many opportunities to respond to needs and challenging situations. Our goal must always be to respond in the most excellent way. Paul gives us great direction in Philippians 2:5: "Your attitude should be the same as that of Christ Jesus."

When you are asked to serve in the children's ministry, realize that God is personally inviting you to become more like his Son. Think about the following situations in which you may one day find yourself, and ask, "What would Jesus do?"

- You greet a first-time visitor who is extremely protective of her child and who needs you to reassure her that her child should really go into your class.

- You greet the reluctant spouse of a disciple whose child does not want to go into class.

- You comfort the child of a single, working mother whose complaint of a stomachache is really just her way of trying to spend some time with her mother.

- You arrive early only to find out that the facility you are using that Sunday is locked and will not be opened for at least half an hour.

These are all real-life situations that have tested my heart. You will face one like these and many more. Each is an opportunity to show Jesus' excellent attitude every time.

To What Degree?

An attitude of excellence does not require a degree in education, theology, medicine or theatre. It does require sacrifice, preparation, imagination and moving out of the old "comfort zone."

If you are an activity teacher, decide that yours will be the best crafts, the greatest games, the most inspiring Life Application, Scripture Memory or Bible Skills centers—the best times together. Decide that your students will leave you in love with and in awe of God. Practice leading each activity at home before attempting to do it in class. Use the Teacher Tips provided in the Kingdom Kids Curriculum or get advice about adapting the activities to your students' differing ability levels. Learn to love what you do—and everyone else is sure to follow.

If you are a lead teacher, think about how you can encourage your teachers as well as your students. Do you have first-time teachers who are new or newly restored disciples? Are they married to nondisciples? Do they have cars? Are they single parents? Do they have physical challenges? Greet them as warmly as you would greet the children. Lead the teachers in your class like Jesus would. Thank them. Invite them to your home. Encourage them with stickers for doing a great job. Lead by your example of excellence in preparation, timeliness and enthusiastic teaching. Earn the respect of the teachers, parents and of the children. Be a great disciple.

First and Last(ing) Impressions

Think about where you begin each class: the registration table. Think about the face that people will see. Will they see Mary or Martha? The Bible says that Jesus looked at a man and loved him

(Mark 10:21). Think about how Jesus would greet each child who comes to your class. In addition to having a peaceful smile and a warm greeting, display your parent letters or the craft-of-the-day on a colorful tablecloth with some flowers or decorations. Make your classroom a welcoming place for parents, teachers and children alike.

Have a Heart

Whether you call the time for the teachers to worship before the children arrive "early communion," "teachers' worship" or just "too early," this time is precious and extremely important and needs to be treated that way. Excellence with our children begins with excellent time with God.

My husband, Tim, and I served as our region's children's ministry leaders for several years. One week Tim noticed a large number of teachers arriving late, so he began giving heart-shaped stickers to those who arrived on time. Before the end of worship, Tim had everyone look around. He challenged those who did not "have a heart" to get a heart for being on time to worship God.

Come to your early worship ready to be filled up spiritually so that you can focus on having the attitude of Jesus—and get ready to be a giver. Have good news ready to share. Offer to help with the communion setup. Bring coffee and muffins for the fellowship.

Talking Trash?

One of the most powerful examples I have seen of a Christlike teacher's attitude is a brother named Joe. Joe served as the "snack center teacher" for our 4-Kindergarten class, with an average of fifty children every Sunday. Week after week, Joe did wonders at snack time. Groups of children were captivated by the way that he threw away their trash! Holding an empty juice box to one ear, Joe would transform this simple piece of garbage into a "telephone" from which he relayed amusing but spiritual messages to the children. Each child (and fellow teacher!) waited in anticipation for what Joe would do next.

Sharing about this experience at a teacher's training workshop, Joe amazed and humbled us all with his childlike spirit as he said, "As I helped these children clean up their messes week after week, I learned how much God has to clean up after me." Joe transformed a role that some would consider less than dignified to display Jesus' attitude of excellence.

Dr. Dave

Another teacher, known to our children's ministry as "Dr. Dave," is a disciple who has also defined excellence in his service with the children. A highly respected pediatrician in our community, he is a coach, mentor, advocate—and a father of two teenagers and a preschooler. His schedule leaves him little room to breathe. But when he is called to serve, Dr. Dave makes no excuses. None. Because of his dedication, preparation and commitment to excellence, every child who passes through his center is amazed, enthralled and wowed by God. One Sunday, Dave set up a full-size tent, and with the help of a flashlight, he created an awe-inspiring setting in which to teach an unforgettable lesson to preschoolers about God!

The Common Denominator

Love is the most excellent way—and Jesus is our flesh and blood example of how to display our love through an attitude of excellence. With this in mind, try this exercise: go back through this chapter and make a list of as many ideas for expressing love as you can—love for children, for other teachers and for God. Use this list as a springboard for ways that you can show your love in your own situation. And, finally, decide to make your attitude of excellence contagious to everyone around you!

A Heart to Change

1. *What have you done to make your class excellent? What more can you do?*
2. *What is your attitude when you are asked to serve in roles such as diaper changer, potty pal or snack helper?*
3. *How have you expressed your love to the other teachers in your class?*
4. *How is God helping you to become more like Jesus through your service with the children?*

Enthusiasm and Excitement

Ben & Beth Weast • Raleigh-Durham, N.C., USA

...for our "God is a consuming fire."

Hebrews 12:29

Our God is a burning fire. He does everything with zeal. Does the creation account in Genesis 1 and 2 read like a technical treatise? How would you describe the Flood and the survival of Noah and his family in the ark? Does God do anything without flair, without zeal? Read the accounts when God scatters those creating the tower of Babel (Genesis 11:1-9), rains burning sulfur on Sodom and Gomorrah (Genesis 19:24), appears in a burning bush (Exodus 3:1-5), parts the Red Sea (Exodus 14:21-22), and tells his laws to Moses and the people on a cloud-covered mountain that was billowing smoke and fire (Exodus 19:18). These are just a few examples that describe the "zeal of the LORD Almighty" (Isaiah 9:7, 37:32) for his name and for his people. Over and over, the Bible displays God's zeal and enthusiasm as he declares to the world that he is its Creator—its King—that his name is to be revered above all names.

There is nothing tepid about the God who seeks to establish a people to be his treasured possession (Deuteronomy 7:6).

God's Zeal for Us

God is filled with zeal for his people because he loves them. Ever since the fall of man, God has zealously pursued us, and his pursuit has been anything but boring. Listen to what Isaiah says:

But now, this is what the Lord says—
he who created you, O Jacob,
he who formed you, O Israel:
"Fear not, for I have redeemed you;
I have summoned you by name; you are mine.
When you pass through the waters,
I will be with you;
and when you pass through the rivers,
they will not sweep over you.
When you walk through the fire,
you will not be burned;
the flames will not set you ablaze.
For I am the Lord, your God,
the Holy One of Israel, your Savior;
I give Egypt for your ransom,
Cush and Seba in your stead.
Since you are precious and honored in my sight,
and because I love you,
I will give men in exchange for you,
and people in exchange for your life. (Isaiah 43:1-4)

Jesus' Zeal

The Son of God is also a burning fire. Some people think that all of the spiritual dramatics ended with the Old Testament's passing. Really? Jesus did everything with zeal. Imagine fasting forty days in a desert and then going head-to-head with the most cunning adversary to ever exist (Matthew 4:1-11). Jesus regenerated the lepers' rotting flesh; he straightened twisted limbs, opened deaf ears and blind eyes, loosened the tongues of the mute, raised the dead, fed thousands from next to nothing, and walked on water. He preached to adoring crowds, yet stood firm in the midst of shouting mobs or when confronted by small groups of the religious elite. Jesus was the perfect teacher. He demonstrated authority never before seen, and as people listened to his message and followed him, their lives were transformed.

Zeal for his Father's house did consume him (Psalm 69:9, John 2:17). He died and was buried, but the greatest light show in history took place as he rose from the dead. Jesus lived and died so that we could "die to sin and live for righteousness" (1 Peter 2:24). He set us free forever. He has zealously pursued us, and his pursuit has been anything but boring. Listen to what Jesus himself says: "I have come that they may have life, and have it to the full" (John 10:10).

Zeal for the Word

Are you, the disciple of Jesus, a teacher of kingdom kids and visitors' children, a burning fire? Do you realize that the Bible is not just a stream of distant memories? It is living and active (Hebrews 4:12)—a fire of its own. The religious and secular worlds have reduced history's greatest action thriller, replete with romantic, comedic and tragic elements, to a monotonous, superficial cartoon. Children come home from denominational Sunday school bored and eager to play the latest video game or watch the Cartoon Network or Nickelodeon.

Anyone with an imagination fueled by the Holy Spirit's fire can lift God's word from the pages of the Bible and create memories for children that will be building blocks in the foundation of what will one day be their complete spiritual house. To become a disciple, you personally fell in love with God's word and with Jesus. As you read and studied, the Bible came alive. You need to remember the zeal with which the disciples presented the Word to you.

Now consider the children you teach. The first step in bringing God's word to life before their eyes is to make sure your heart burns with zeal for God and his word. David says,

> The statutes you have laid down are righteous;
>   they are fully trustworthy.
> My zeal wears me out,
>   for my enemies ignore your words.
> Your promises have been thoroughly tested,
>   and your servant loves them. (Psalm 119:138-140)

Paul says,

> It is fine to be zealous, provided the purpose is good, and to be so always and not just when I am with you. (Galatians 4:18)

> Never be lacking in zeal, but keep your spiritual fervor, serving the Lord. (Romans 12:11)

There is no better purpose for being zealous than making disciples. This is what you are doing as you teach the children. Wear yourself out praying for God to fill your heart with zeal for his word and for him to fill your mind with creative ways to bring it alive before the children.

Zealous Imitation

The second step is to look at the greatest teacher who ever lived, and zealously imitate his Spirit-filled creativity. Become a master storyteller. Jesus was. Put together true-to-life illustrations that your children will recognize and embrace. Jesus did it with parables. Our generation is blessed with incredible technology. Use everything that is available to you to burn the message of God into the hearts of your children. Jesus did. He used boats, seeds, small groups, mud, home-made whips, fingers, fish and swords. We have video cameras, CD players, VCRs and more. Instead of lamenting that too many high-tech gimmicks influence our children, use the technology to support your teaching. This is what Jesus would do.

Whether you are an accomplished teacher or a beginner who fumbles and stumbles does not matter to the children you teach. Children respond to spiritual energy. This means more than you and the children bouncing around like pinballs and yelling the whole time. Even in the quiet moments of the class, they will see the Spirit's gleam twinkling in the smile of your eyes. They will hear him in the resolve of your voice. They will respond because your heart radiates a burning love for God and his gracious salvation. They will respond because God will call them through you.

A Heart to Change

1. *Does God's love and zeal for you inspire you? How are your personal times with God inspiring you? If they aren't, get advice and get a plan for how you can change.*
2. *Would the children and other teachers in your class describe you as "a burning fire" or "tepid" in the way that you present God and his word to them? What can you change in your presentation to make God's word come alive as you teach?*
3. *How can you better imitate Jesus in his creativity and energy?*

THIS IS MY COMMANDMENT

Discipling One Another in Children's Ministry

Barry & Nancy Lamb • London, UK

> Instead, speaking the truth in love, we will in all things grow up into him who is the Head, that is, Christ. From him the whole body, joined and held together by every supporting ligament, grows and builds itself up in love, as each part does its work.
>
> *Ephesians 4:15-16*

As God's kingdom advances into the twenty-first century, significant specialized ministries will continue to develop and build as the needs of the church are discovered and met. The key to any ministry, however, will always be the strength of the relationships that are built within it. In other words—discipling.

One Body

Paul taught the Corinthian church that we all have roles in the church. Loving discipling helps us fulfill these roles while all pulling in the same direction for the same purpose—glorifying God, becoming more like Jesus, making disciples and serving the church. We all have different strengths, but working together benefits the whole. When people are fulfilled—doing something they are naturally gifted to do—they normally live a more fruitful life. One brother in London had not been evangelistically fruitful for seven years when he came into children's ministry as a lead teacher. Within a year he was fruitful in his evangelism three times. The discipling he received in the children's ministry made a big difference in the rest of his life.

In March 1995 our ministry leader asked us to oversee the children's ministry in the East sector of the London church on a short-term basis. This role was a long way from our hearts, but we agreed with the (arrogant) understanding that it would be temporary. We were at that time would-be family group leaders, far from fulfilling our potential, but God had a lesson in store for us. The leader moved on to another sector shortly afterward; we have stayed with the children's ministry to this day.

It was in the children's ministry where I (Nancy) learned to give my heart. Often, we can understand the *principles* of loving and caring, but miss out at the heart level. I began to think about the needs of the children's ministry constantly: How can we inspire disciples to embrace teaching? What can we do for parents with children who will not settle down? How can we motivate the teachers to put every effort into preparing classes? I had at last found a role that pushed me to give wholeheartedly, and yet if it were up to me, I would never have volunteered for it.

Five years later, we are on the ministry staff, leading the children's ministry for the churches in the United Kingdom and have an incredible leadership group. All this has come about because we were open to advice about where we could best serve.

One Another

Creating a team spirit is essential. Everyone needs to feel valued, useful and appreciated. Friday night discipleship groups, led by John Partington (one of the elders in London) and his wife, Rose, were helpful not only for getting us excited about children's ministry, but also for getting our hearts right as disciples. We are extremely blessed to have the elders and sector leaders supporting children's ministry family groups with permanent teachers within them. This means seven children's ministry coordinators oversee family groups consisting of more than ninety dedicated lead teachers. As coordinators, we have grown together, supporting and encouraging one another. Incredibly, God has raised up five of the London coordinators to be elders in training.

The coordinators value unity with their sector leaders. They appreciate the focus of their leaders while ensuring that the needs of the children's ministry are not overlooked. Where possible, they personally are discipled by ministry staff, so they are able to speak up and be heard.

Within the family groups, we encourage married couples to teach one age group and to work with other marrieds in discipling partnerships. This dynamic helps couples learn to work together in their classrooms as well as in their marriages. The single disciples can expect great discipling partnerships too. Bunmi Adebajo has taught in Kingdom Kids for more than four years and disciples two lead teachers. All teach the two and three year olds. Together, they have created an excellent standard within their classroom, while maintaining a caring friendship outside with each other. One of the teachers, Anne-Marie, was fruitful in evangelism twice last month. These young disciples, met by Anne-Marie, formed important early bonding relationships with another non-Kingdom Kids family group in their geographic area to receive the support they would need.

Appreciation is crucial. We recently started having workshops for the teachers of each individual children's age group in London. We also have a two-day retreat at the end of the year for all the permanent lead teachers and coordinators. Teachers come away refreshed spiritually and inspired to serve again.

One Mission

Support is always a two-way street. The more the sector leaders feel that the specialized ministries are focused on reaching out and converting the lost, the happier they are to provide the best people for the job. The expectation for seeking and saving the lost in a Kingdom Kids family group is the same as in any other ministry. Time spent each week preparing classes and getting involved in the lives of the children should not prevent lifestyle evangelism, and a continual focus on converting the lost keeps disciples on the cutting edge, delivering classes that are real to our children. Then the kingdom kids themselves can have the faith to believe that God will bless them as much as anyone else. In fact, the Kingdom Kids family groups in London have consistently been some of the most evangelistically fruitful ministries. At the time of writing, our seven Kingdom Kids family groups have met and helped twenty people become Christians the last sixty days.

Just as the supporting ligaments are essential within the human body for it to function effectively, so it is with Christ's body. We must make sure the ligaments are not pulling in different directions but working together, supporting one another. When this happens, our mission as disciples will never be overlooked or neglected.

Discipling is more than a command; it is the only effective tool to pull the body together to provide the church with the heart and support it needs to grow and build specialized ministries up in love, as each disciple within that ministry does his or her work.

A Heart to Change

1. *Are you getting advice from your leaders, other teachers and parents about how you can have the maximum impact in your discipling relationships and with the children you serve?*
2. *Do you see your class as your ministry in which you can spur others on toward love and good deeds? What can you do to show your appreciation for the children and for the other teachers?*
3. *How can you grow in your personal effectiveness and teamwork by seeking and saving the lost while you serve in the children's ministry?*

I WANT TO BE A WORKER FOR THE LORD

Staying Tied In

Kim Evans • Philadelphia, USA

> Then Jesus came to them and said, "All authority in heaven and on earth has been given to me. Therefore go and make disciples of all nations, baptizing them in the name of the Father and of the Son and of the Holy Spirit, and teaching them to obey everything I have commanded you. And surely I am with you always, to the very end of the age."
>
> *Matthew 28:18-20*

When you are serving in the children's ministry, it is easy to get disconnected from the broader ministry of the church. Your role with the children is vital, but if you neglect other needs in the body, you will suffer and so will the church. It is important for every children's ministry worker to remember that for all Christians, our ministry remains the same—to go and make disciples, teaching them to obey everything...." Some things just don't change, even though you are taking your turn in children's ministry. Our job is to stay close to God, to love others (including the children we serve and the parents who bring them) and to keep seeking and saving the lost.

Overcome the Challenges

Satan loves to get us distracted doing good things so that we will completely forget about our mission. He enlarges problems in our minds to make them look insurmountable. He feeds us lies, like telling us that people will not want to come to church with us while we are in children's ministry because we can't sit with them. Don't fall into these traps. Sure, there are challenges, but look for ways to overcome them. Ask those in your ministry group to sit with your visitors and to make sure they are drawn into the fellowship. Have your visitors stop by your class to see you. (It is not a time for fellowship, but they will be inspired by what they see.) We are happiest when we bring people to church, study the Bible with them and help them to make Jesus their Lord.

Build Relationships with Parents

Pray for opportunities to reach out to families with children in the age group that you teach. Children beg their parents to come back to church—or beg to never come back—based on their Kingdom Kids experience. Our curriculum is such a powerful tool to draw the children to God and therefore to draw families. Some of my favorite conversations have resulted from talking with non-Christian parents about the impact and the fun of children's ministry. Encourage the children in your class to bring their friends.

Your own personal fellowship is a vital part of your spiritual well-being. It takes more effort while you are teaching to get this needed fellowship, but you can make it happen. Use times before and after church to meet up with people. Realize how crucial the other services are to both meeting your needs and the needs of others. Build new relationships and make new memories with the children and their parents and with the other teachers. The best way to win parents' hearts is through loving their children—and you will develop relationships that you would never have had except through your willingness to serve.

Make Your Worship Meaningful

If you are teaching on Sunday, be certain that the communion is the central focus of your worship. Arrive early for fellowship so that you can slow down and really focus on your fellowship with God. Communion should not be a legalistic time that you rush into and then squeeze in before you begin teaching. It is our time to remember Christ and his death, burial and resurrection. These times of worship are vital. Never think of them as optional. When you walk in to serve our children, you need to have come from a time with God where you truly worshiped him and drew his strength for your task.

Don't Lose Touch

I would also urge you to do whatever it takes to stay current with what is happening with the rest of the church. Get copies of the announcements and arrange to get notes and cassettes of the sermons or classes that you miss.

Many of you serve in some form of leadership in addition to your teaching responsibilities. Seek advice about how to plan and fit it all in from those who have been successful at it so that you do not neglect your other responsibilities. For instance, I would not recommend that someone who leads a family group and their assistant teach simultaneously. It is difficult to meet the needs of the family group. We are the family of God, and we need to meet the needs of both the children and the adults. Also, stay tuned in and know what is happening in your discipling relationships. It absolutely takes more work, but it can be done.

Your time in children's ministry will be a busy time. Meeting the needs of the children and staying tied in to everything else will stretch you. But my final encouragement is to love every minute you are with the children. Love the families who love the children and share all of your memories, fun and lessons. Enjoy!

A Heart to Change

1. *What are your expectations for your personal spiritual growth while serving in the children's ministry?*
2. *What weaknesses in you are revealed by working with the children? Do you typically slow down in sharing your faith or in your personal fellowship when you serve in the children's ministry? What key decisions do you need to make to stay in tune with your larger ministry during this time?*
3. *What other disciples will be the biggest help in keeping you tied in to the broader ministry of the church while you are serving the children?*
4. *What is your greatest joy in serving the children?*

14
I'M FIGHTIN' ON THE LORD'S SIDE

Shaping the Next Generation

Sheridan Wright • New York City, USA

These commandments that I give you today are to be
upon your hearts. Impress them on your children.
Deuteronomy 6:6-7a

"Only time will tell." When was the last time you heard someone use that phrase? Was it in reference to a relationship or a promise or some great endeavor? Perhaps it came from a cynical or skeptical mind. Even so, it still is a great challenge that needs to be considered, especially in reference to the great movement we are part of. In the first century, Gamaliel expressed this same "wait and see" sentiment to his fellow Sanhedrin members when he urged them to let the apostles go (Acts 5:38-39). He knew that time would tell whether this "movement" was of God or man. So it is with us today.

Will our movement be a mere footnote in religious history about a group of dreamers who claimed to want to be used by God but were unable to pass our dreams on to the next generation? Or will we submit to Jesus' purpose: "I chose you and appointed you to go and bear fruit— fruit that will last" (John 15:16). Inherent in the Great Commission is the expectation for all disciples to not only make disciples of their own generation, but to make disciples of the succeeding generations as well. If you belong to Jesus, then this is your heart. And this being so, time will not be a challenge, but a verification for our entire movement.

To be sure, God has given the primary responsibility for shaping the next generation to parents. This has always been his plan.

However, he has made the church and its children's ministry the secondary influence. Unfortunately, in some situations where a family is not what God intends for it to be, the children's ministry becomes the sole influence. Children form their ideas about God from their parents and their ideas about church from the children's ministry. No child should ever have to overcome unpleasant or boring memories about church in order to become a disciple. This would be an insult to God. As a teacher, what you do in the children's ministry does count and has a direct bearing on the faith of the next generation. This needs to compel us to approach the planning and teaching of classes and activities with the utmost zeal and commitment, with no tolerance for mediocrity and halfheartedness. The children deserve our best!

We will only give our best to our children if we have a living faith—a faith that is genuine, full of vision and focused on pleasing God and not men.

Genuine Faith

First, our faith must be genuine. When Jesus condemned the hypocrites in Matthew 23, one of the first areas he addressed was that they didn't live what they preached (Matthew 13:1-3). This has a devastating effect on anyone, but especially on children. They can tell if someone really believes what they are teaching or not. They relate by feeling and not by correct wording, so they can "feel" empty, faithless words. This produces the effects mentioned in Proverbs 13:12: their hope is deferred and their hearts grow sick when they don't see power in the lives of those who are instructing them.

For example, teachers cannot merely teach children about evangelizing the world. They need to share about individuals they have led and are leading to Jesus. They cannot merely teach about the power of God, but they need to share how God's power is causing them personally to change and grow. They cannot merely teach about loving each other, but they need to share about the closeness and openness of their own relationships in the body of Christ. We cannot pass on what we are not.

Children's ministry has never been an "escape" from the responsibilities of being a disciple, such as evangelism, growing spiritually and building one-another relationships. The command of God to parents in Deuteronomy 6:6-7 is a principle that needs to be obeyed by anyone who teaches. If we are personally experiencing what we are teaching, then the children's hearts will be filled with the hope that God is not only real but greater than any obstacles they face—and they will be inspired to seek him.

Long-Range Vision

Second, our faith must manifest itself in vision. In shaping the next generation, we need a vision that rises above the disappointments, problems and challenges of today and sees what can be tomorrow. It is important to remember the big picture. Remember that the children's ministry leads to the preteen ministry, which leads to the teen ministry, which leads to the campus ministry, which produces leaders and bolsters the adult ministry. The degree to which we understand the importance of this chain will determine how well we do our part in the children's ministry.

There will be plenty of times when, despite your prayers and effort, you will face discouragement because it just doesn't seem like anything is getting through. The children will seem to care more about what others think rather than what God thinks. We *cannot* lose heart at this point! We need to pray for ourselves the same prayer Elisha prayed for his servant: "O Lord, open [our] eyes so that [we] may see!" (2 Kings 6:17). The servant saw the working of God in this desperate situation, and we too can step back and see the larger picture.

Jesus promised in Mark 4:26-29, that the kingdom of God is like a seed that is planted and grows though we do not know how. We need to have the vision to see this in the hearts of our children. Even though they may seem disinterested, we need to be diligent and consistent in planting the word of God in their hearts. This "disinterest" is merely a mask for anger, hurt or fear. However, the word of God is more powerful and will grow and bear fruit. Open your eyes and see this and remain diligent, for God is at work, raising up another generation.

God Pleasers

Finally, we need to have a faith that seeks the approval of God rather than man. There is absolutely nothing wrong with encouraging and being encouraged. This is very Biblical and necessary. However, our "bottom line" cannot be that we do things to be noticed by others. Often we can find ourselves in a real battle for our hearts because our flesh seeks to be noticed and praised by others. When this doesn't happen, we can begin to brood, and our hearts can become filled with pettiness and resentment. True disciples win this battle (Galatians 1:10). If they get praised, fine. If they don't, fine. They live to hear the words from the Father, "Well done, good and faithful servant" (Matthew 25: 21, 23).

The children's ministry does not produce the immediate "results" seen in other ministries. Baptisms are years in the making at this point. We need to serve the children wholeheartedly with joy because we know that God is pleased and that he is using us to shape his next generation. If this is your faith, then I can promise you a gift. It will happen in the future at a service or a conference or a fellowship. You will see some of these same children whom you labored for, as adults, serving and leading in the kingdom of God with conviction. At that moment, your heart will be filled with that special joy John spoke about in 3 John 4: "I have no greater joy than to hear that my children are walking in the truth." This will be a gift and kiss from God. Only time will tell? Absolutely!

A Heart to Change

1. *What is the current state of your faith? What scriptures did you use to make this assessment? Ask a few spiritual friends whether or not they agree with how you see your faith.*
2. *Think about the recent baptisms in your congregation or region. Have any of them been teens who spent most of their younger years in the children's ministry? (If you don't know of any, be sure to ask around to see if there have been any.) How can this vision keep your teaching fresh?*
3. *What are your primary motivations for wanting to do a great job serving in the children's ministry?*
4. *Imagine that Jesus (as a child) was in your class. How would your teaching change? Matthew 25:44-45 is not about children's ministry, but is there a principle here for you to apply as you work with the kingdom kids?*

PART 2

Tools and Resources

15
UNDERSTANDING THE CENTER APPROACH

Clegg & Betty Dyson • Raleigh-Durham, N.C., USA

Variety is said to be the spice of life. This applies no less to children than to adults. Activity centers are an exciting way to teach children while giving them variety and change of activity in order to prevent boredom.

The activity center approach is excellent for less experienced teachers because it sets them up for success and makes the number of children manageable. Thus, the children are able to learn in an exciting way with far fewer behavior problems. Sounds almost too good to be true, doesn't it? Well, believe it—it's true!

Before Going to the Centers

Before the centers begin, the children will arrive at the designated area for registration. After they have been registered, they will be escorted by an adult to a Preclass Activity area. Children should have several activities to choose from, including at least one provided in the lesson. Children will do their preclass activities until the class is ready to begin.

Dividing into Centers

The way centers work is quite simple: three activity centers are established. Depending on the age of your class and whether it is the Core or Supplement Lesson, these centers may be: Bible Story, Life Application, Craft, Game, Scripture Memory (or Bible Skills, depending upon the age group). A large room works very well since each corner of the room can be designated for a particular center. Each center should be clearly indicated with a large, colorful sign.

A teacher is assigned to each center and is responsible for preparing that center's activity. During each class session, he or she will repeat the center's activity for each group of children.

Grouping the Children

After preclass, the lead teacher gathers the children together for a welcome, singing and review of the rules. The teacher then counts the number of children and divides by the number of centers. For example, in a class with twenty-four children and three activity centers, there will be three groups of eight children. The lead teacher will send a group of children to each of the three activity centers where they will spend ten to twenty minutes (depending on age) and then move to a different center.

In classes where children are in a combined age group, try to divide the small groups by ages. For example, in a 4s and 5s class, try to group children of the same age together. This helps the activity center teachers to address their different developmental needs.

Time in Each Center

Each center is allotted a certain amount of time. The time is determined by dividing the amount of class time into three equal segments. This does not include time spent waiting for the children to arrive or the actual transition of children to their next center. Also allow time at the end for the children to return to the specific area where they will be picked up by their parents. Here are some examples of class schedules:

The lead teacher gives the center teachers a five-minute "warning" to close out their activity and prepare children to rotate. When it is time to change centers, the children will be asked to quietly form a single line and move with an adult to the next center. For younger children, have them "make a train" to walk to the next center.

Snack: The Fourth Center?

In churches where classes number more than thirty children, you may want to create a fourth center for snack. In this case, the lead teacher divides the entire group into four smaller groups and rotates them through four different centers: three activity centers and a snack center. If this is necessary for your class, you will have to manage your timetable to allow adequate time for all four centers.

Class Schedule for Sunday Worship at 10:00 am	Class Schedule for Midweek Service at 7:30 pm
9:30 to 10:20 Preclass Activity	7:00 to 7:40 Preclass Activity
10:20 to 10:35 Welcome, singing, rules review, division of children into small groups	7:40 to 7:50 Welcome, singing, rules review, division of children into small groups
10:40 to 11:05 Center #1	7:55 to 8:15 Center #1
11:10 to 11:35 Center #2	8:15 to 8:35 Center #2
11:40 to 12:00 Center #3	8:35 to 9:00 Center #3
12:00 To parent pickup—post-class activities: preclass or review of lesson activities	9:00 To parent pickup—post-class activities: preclass or review of lesson activities

Advantages of Centers

Behavior problems are significantly reduced in centers due to the small group setting and the adult to child ratio. In large classes, centers help increase children's safety by ensuring that teachers are focused on one particular group of children at all times. The twenty-minute activity periods help children achieve greater focus—avoiding boredom and trouble. Changing groups, seeing different teachers and having new activities at each center is exciting to the children. The result is much better behavior.

Teachers, regardless of their experience with children, can do a great job teaching an activity center. With the help of these lessons, any disciple who follows the directions can lead fun, age-appropriate and engaging activities for any age group.

This chapter was adapted from *Heroes* by Clegg and Betty Dyson (Woburn, Mass.: Discipleship Publications International, 1993).

16
INSPIRATIONAL TEACHING

Theresa Ferguson • Boston, USA

Deep in the heart of all teachers should be the compelling desire to make a real difference in the lives of their students. Thinking back through my life, as I was taught about God, Jesus and the Bible as a child, I recall with great appreciation certain teachers who made an eternal impact on my heart. They did not view teaching children as a menial task that someone had to do; they saw it as an opportunity to plant spiritual seeds that would produce fruit for a lifetime and change the destinies of souls. The end result in my life was far-reaching indeed. I majored in elementary education in college and taught in the public school system. I taught Bible classes in a traditional church for many years and taught my own children daily as long as they lived with me. (Now I am teaching my grandchildren!) I was deeply involved in developing the Kingdom Kids Curriculum and then personally teaching it in the children's ministry of the Boston church. My teachers inspired me to teach.

Can you think of teachers who had a similar impact on your heart and life? Take some time to think about it as you read this chapter. If you can think of such teachers, you can be sure that they were inspirational teachers. Those who were not are quickly forgotten, as are the lessons that they taught. Being *effective* teachers demands that we are *inspirational* teachers. This is not an option.

Imitating the Master

Inspirational teaching—what is it? According to the dictionary, to inspire others means "to fill with an animating, quickening or exalting influence; to influence or impel; to animate, as an influence, feeling, thought or the like, does; to prompt or instigate by influence." For us, it means that we have imitated Jesus enough to teach like he taught. And it also means that we have imitated effective teachers he has put in our lives.

What can we learn from Jesus, the Master Teacher? He was inspired by God to the point that he totally loved the word of God and the people for whom it was written. He so loved the message of God that he made it come alive to all who heard his teaching. All inspirational teaching begins with a teacher who loves God, God's word and the ones whom he or she is laboring to teach. In the practicals of teaching, Jesus was unexcelled. The task of the teacher is to know the subject well enough to break it down into easily understood parts and to make the presentation captivating. Look how Jesus did this.

1. He used simple illustrations from everyday life.
2. He asked many questions, both to prompt thinking and to see if he was being understood.
3. He made applications and called for responses.
4. He demonstrated his teaching, as in the case when he washed the disciples' feet (John 13).

Without doubt, Jesus labored to make God's message clearly understood. How much effort do you make in planning your lessons to ensure that you are both practical and inspirational? Such teaching does not just happen. It comes at a price, and we must be willing to pay the price.

Lasting Impact

Don't ever doubt the difference you can make. The most exciting and inspiring teacher I can remember from my childhood had an amazing impact on me at age eight. In fact, my desire to help others know God traces back to what she said in only one presentation to my class. She made me believe that sharing God's word was the most important thing anyone could possibly do with their lives. I can still remember much of what inspired me from just that one class. She captured the attention of the class by turning out the lights in the room and holding a candle to provide light. She entered the room dressed like a woman from the country about which she was sharing. She acted out what she would do in that country to share Jesus with the children there, and then urged us to share with our friends, making the point that unless we shared, they would never know about Jesus. I made a decision that day in response to her inspiring presentation that has stayed with me until this very day, and now God is helping me carry out that dream, even to the point of teaching people in other countries about him.

Note the inspirational principles that this teacher used so effectively.

1. She made sure that our eyes, hearts and minds were drawn into her presentation.
2. Her dress provided a very effective visual aid to help us connect with the situation she described.
3. Her words were brief but appropriate for the age level and were delivered with dramatic intensity and conviction.
4. She made her message applicable to us in a way that left us knowing exactly how to put it into practice in our lives.
5. She held the Bible so that we all could see it, and the way she handled it made us realize its exalted importance.
6. She instilled confidence in us that God had a plan for our lives and would use us to change the world.
7. Finally, she called for a decision and response to her lesson.

That I remember so much detail about her convictions, her life and her presentation for almost half a century shows the power of a teacher to inspire and change the lives of impressionable children.

Practicals

Let me close by giving you some practical and specific "how-to's" for teaching our kingdom kids today.

1. Remember that seventy percent of your influence as a teacher will be the manner of your interaction with the children. Do you love them, and are you making it real and fun?
2. Prepare your mind and heart by letting the Bible inspire you. Read the story you are going to present many times, visualizing it in your mind to make it come alive to you and then thinking of how to make it come alive to your students.
3. Pray for each child every day by name. Keep a list of their names handy in your Bible.
4. Realize that spirits communicate with spirits, which means that the children (even the very young) will definitely sense how important they are to you and how important effective communication with them actually is. Your excitement and personal involvement will make or break the effectiveness of the class.

5. Think about the kind of preaching and teaching that inspires and motivates you most, and pattern your own teaching after these same principles that others use effectively.
6. Understand that inspiring the children actually begins with your initial greeting of the children as they enter the class. Eye contact and the use of exciting, encouraging words set the stage for the rest of the class. In the preclass portion, asking the children about their day and making personalized comments about their feelings or appearance helps to pull them in emotionally. ("Johnny, I am so happy to see you today. We are going to have such an exciting Bible story about Jonah!")
7. In presenting the Bible Story section, the use of animation with exaggerated movement of the arms, hands and eyes is absolutely essential for gaining and keeping attention. Self-denial and focusing on the children will help you to lose your own inhibitions and self-consciousness.
8. Appeal to their five senses (Smell, taste, sight, hearing and touch) to keep them involved in what you are communicating. Food to smell and taste, bright colored pictures to see, action songs to sing and hear, and toys and visuals to touch are all effective ways to keep yourself and the children animated and connected emotionally.
9. Make the most of every opportunity, realizing that every minute can be used to influence the children toward spiritual values that will change their lives.
10. Use the Scriptures. Keep the Bible open and let the children interact with the Bible.
11. Use personal examples, stating your love for God and the Bible and calling on the other teachers to do the same. Asking the teachers, "Do you love the Bible?" will provide a model for the students to imitate.
12. Call the children to a decision by asking them for a reply—"Are you going to love Jesus and tell others about him?"
13. Encourage and inspire the other teachers and workers in your age group. For example, having a meal once per month at the beginning of a new unit to prepare for the new lessons or new students will build a sense of team and family.

What an opportunity we all have! In any given class we can do and say things that children will remember for a lifetime. Let us pray that we will not waste these precious opportunities but will make an inspiring imprint on the young hearts and minds that are entrusted to us.

17
THE ROLE OF ASSISTANT TEACHERS

Rob Davis • Boston, USA

For I know your eagerness to help, and I have been boasting about it to the Macedonians, telling them that since last year you in Achaia were ready to give; and your enthusiasm has stirred most of them to action.

2 Corinthians 9:2

Being eager to help is a quality that God recognizes and affirms. There is nothing second rate about helping. Many of you will be serving in the children's ministry as assistant teachers. In this role you will be there to provide help to the lead teachers and to the students. As you prepare for your service, ask yourself these questions: Do I know what it means to help? Do I know what it *takes* to help? Do I really *want* to help in a great way?

These are important questions because great assistant teachers are key in having a great Bible class and a great children's ministry. In your role as an assistant teacher you will be, for the lead teacher, extra eyes, hands and a singing voice. For the children you will be a friend and role model. But what kind of role model will you be? Will the children see your passion for God and for the Bible, or will they just see you "putting in your time," taking your turn in the children's ministry? Each week, will they see you focus your attention on them or on checking your watch? Will your class be something they eagerly look forward to? By deciding to be like Jesus in your energy level, your initiative and your love for the children, you will help to build a children's ministry that will prepare young hearts and minds to call Jesus Lord.

Energy

Children want to have fun. In fact, children expect to be bombarded by fun. The Internet, Nickelodeon, Game Boy, Nintendo, Happy Meal toys, Radio Disney—these are your competitors for their attention. If you are either concerned with looking foolish or you simply will not expend the energy to be exciting, you will lose. The Bible tells us that children loved to be with Jesus; they chose to be with him rather than be occupied with the distractions of their day. Why? Because he died to himself and was able to capture their interest.

You must reach out and grab the attention of the children. Do this with bright clothes, high energy, a big smile and a zany attitude. Loosen up. Have fun. Be out of yourself. When it is time to sing "Who's the King of the Jungle?"—do it with zeal; put your whole body into it. When you are asked to play Moses and lead the Israelites out of Egypt, raise your staff with vigor and holler, "Follow me!" Whether you are helping with snacks, singing along with the children or listening to the Bible story, be wholeheartedly involved. If you are not excited to be there, why should they be? "Never be lacking in zeal, but keep your spiritual fervor, serving the Lord" (Romans 12:11). Ask yourself, "Is God pleased with my energy level?"

Initiative

Do you want to make God and your lead teacher very happy? Take the initiative. I have been the lead teacher, and I have been an assistant teacher, and I understand both perspectives. As the lead teacher, I was concerned with every aspect of the class and felt the responsibility to make the class great. However, in the midst of overseeing the lesson and the assistant teachers and the students, I was often unable to address every issue as it arose. I needed assistant teachers who wanted as much as I did to have an excellent class.

The best classes happen when every adult decides to look for ways to make it great. Make the decision that you are going to be the extra eyes, ears and hands for the lead teacher. *You* be the one to bring Billy back to the group when he wanders away; *you* help Mary with the arm movements to "Building Up the Kingdom," *you* help Johnny to listen when the teacher is telling the Bible story—without being asked. Take the initiative; don't just put your time in. Ask yourself, "Is God pleased with my initiative?"

Love

The Bible teaches that love is patient—not self-seeking, not easily angered—and love never fails (1 Corinthians 13). Do you love Jimmy, even though week after week he does not do the craft and talks much more than he listens? Do you want Rachel to grow up to be a disciple, having great memories of her Bible class, or do you want class to hurry and end so you can get to lunch quickly? These examples may sound silly, but these are thoughts I have wrestled with. Love is not natural; it takes dying to yourself.

Jimmy and Rachel probably have enough clanging cymbals (1 Corinthians 13:1) in their lives; what they need is your love. Children in the first century were confident of Jesus' love. Are the children in your class confident of yours? Are you warm? Are you patient? Do you put in the effort to know the children? Do you know what to expect from their age group? Do you study the children to learn what they need, to know what will make the class a great experience for each of them? It's hard to imagine being more like God than when we are loving children. Of course, the converse to that statement is also true. Make a decision to die to yourself and love the children under your care. Periodically ask yourself, "Is God pleased with my love for the children?"

The Difference

I have taught many classes as the lead teacher, and for the most part I feel like I do a good job. I remember one first and second grade class in particular that was consistently excellent. The children behaved well and participated, registration went smoothly—as did the transition between centers—and the time seemed to fly by each week. I was thinking I was a pretty awesome lead teacher until a year later, when I had quite a different experience. My stress level was higher, I felt like I was running all over the class putting out fires, and I was exhausted each week by the end of class. I realized then that what was great about my previous class was not so much me as the teacher, but my assistant teachers and their sincere desire to do their best to establish an excellent class. Do the same in your class. Give everything you can to make it exceptional!

18
RELATING TO CHILDREN

Sue Anderson • Washington, D.C., USA

Think about how you go about studying the Bible with someone to help him or her become a Christian. What if you were a married person with several children, in your late thirties, studying the Bible with a college student? Let's say this non-Christian is a good fifteen to twenty years younger than you. How effective would you be if all your examples were centered on your life as a parent, your financial concerns, your life at work and so on. This poor non-Christian would struggle to try to relate to your life. Instead, wouldn't you make the effort to remember back to college days—what your life was like, what pressures you felt, what your concerns were and the major temptations that you faced? You would do this in order to relate the Bible to that person's life—making it more real to them and thus more convicting and impacting.

On Their Level

How much more so do we need to work at relating the Bible to children. In the example above, college students may have the mental capacity to envision themselves as parents, thus relating the Bible to their lives. Children, however, are mentally and emotionally unable to engage in this higher level of thinking. As teachers, we must become masterful at relating the spiritual truths of God, Jesus and his word to the children at their level, so that they understand them.

We are very fortunate to have the Kingdom Kids Curriculum that virtually does this for us. All lessons have been written and often scripted for a particular age group. I have seen, however, classes taught in a manner that goes right above the children's heads. One clear practical: It is fairly easy to engage the attention of children. If you are looking at a lot of blank stares and shuffling bodies, you are not relating to them. They are lost somewhere. You need to find them and bring them back.

You may be thinking, *But how?* Perhaps you are a college student, a single professional or you are married and either have no children or your children are grown. The world of children may be far from your everyday life. You have been asked to be the lead teacher or assistant teacher for a class of eighteen kindergartners. You feel insecure in having the responsibility of teaching God's word to these five-year-old boys and girls. Don't worry; you are in good company. I have seen the most fearless preachers in the kingdom struggle with insecurity at the thought of being a ministry director at our summer camp—for children ages eight to fourteen.

The great things about children, however, are their openness, honesty and true love for learning. They are like sponges—taught at their level, they soak up and retain much. You are embarking on an exciting adventure.

Proven Principles

As you focus on relating to children and teaching on their level, here are some principles I have seen proven in my own work in the children's ministry.

Investigate

Talk to a child in the age group you are teaching. Find out what he or she enjoys doing. What does he or she like talking about? Better yet, take time in your first class to ask questions of this nature. Listen carefully to the children's answers; what is their world like?

If you are teaching older children or the preteen class, it is imperative that you get to know their world. Ask them what television shows, movies and music they enjoy the most, then watch or listen to them. This will really tell you a lot about them. Try to incorporate what you have learned of their world into class. Many children spend most of their days in school. Find out what is going on in school. Ask them lots of questions.

Tell Relatable Stories

Jesus taught many spiritual truths in parables. One reason he did this was to relate spiritual truths to the everyday life situations of his listeners. Another reason was so that they could remember. Children generally are not interested in facts and figures, but real life examples will always stick.

For example, I taught a lesson recently to my class about Jesus healing the man with leprosy. My husband and I had taken a trip to India the previous year and were able to visit the HOPE Worldwide leprosy village. I brought in pictures of people whose physical appearance showed this disease. There were many "Ohhhs" and "Ahhhs"— and we were able to have a great discussion in which the children were fully engaged. You may not have gone to India, but you surely can go to the library, check out a few books and bring them into the class.

Use current events to teach Biblical truths. The children tend to be aware of big news events, which can be a great opportunity to teach how the Bible can help us make sense of our world.

Apply the Bible

Once you are getting into their world and once you have their attention, help them see how the Bible applies to the things they deal with. Help them see how the Bible applies to their experiences at school. Especially show them how to apply the Scriptures at home. What were the struggles and challenges in your family when you were a child, in your relationships with your siblings and your parents? Children face those same issues today. Many children have challenging home situations. You can teach them how the Bible can help them and give them guidance and direction.

Just prior to this writing I had the opportunity to speak with an eight-year-old girl who was having a difficult time in her relationship with her stepfather, who had recently become a Christian. It was so great to open the Bible and show her Ephesians 6:1-3. She learned that God expected her to honor her father and mother and that God would bless her life if she obeyed him. What a great thing it is to show children what the Bible says to them!

Give Appropriate Instructions

Be sure to give direction and to talk to the children on their level. I have seen teachers explain the directions for the day's craft to younger children, and then say, "Go!"—and the children have no clue what to do. Be sure you know their level of certain skills, such as reading and writing. This may vary within a certain grade level, but at least you will not expect a first grader to read like a fourth grader.

The world of children is very simple, yet dynamic. Things happen to change them daily. It is great to see children mature. Those who teach the two and three year olds know that there is a large difference between a two-year-old and an almost-four-year-old. Children begin kindergarten not being able to read or write and within a year can do both. Preteens seem to change before your very eyes. What a privilege it is to make God, Jesus and his word relatable to the children!

19
CLASS MANAGEMENT

Clegg & Betty Dyson • Raleigh-Durham, N.C., USA

Have you ever walked into a class where children were practically bouncing off the walls, the teacher was frazzled and frantic, and absolutely no learning was going on? Although you certainly do not want to rule your students with an iron hand, you do need to have a sense of order. Through prayer, planning and preparation, you can do much to set the kind of calm and peaceful environment that will help your students learn. The more prepared you are, the fewer discipline problems you will have. Generally speaking, an unprepared teacher is an insecure teacher. And an insecure teacher is more apt to go to one extreme or the other: yelling loudly to gain control or being so structured as to stifle fun and creativity.

In the Beginning

After you have done all you can do to prepare for the class and the children have gathered to begin, it is time to communicate your expectations to the children. This too will help create the order you want for the class. Just like their adult counterparts, children want to know the plan for the day and what you expect from them. Talk to the children about the lesson, the songs you want to sing, and the exciting crafts and games. With great enthusiasm and joy give them a preview of what is to come. If you are excited, the children will be excited.

Once the plan has been discussed with the children, let them know the rules or guidelines they need to follow to make the class a success. It is also important to help them understand the role of discipline in the class if they are not willing to participate according to the set rules or guidelines.

Using the center approach that is called for in the Kingdom Kids Curriculum helps to maintain order in the class. (See chapter 15 to understand the center approach.) Each child is engaged in a small group activity, so there is more accountability and more focus and attention from the teacher to hold the child's interest.

To help you have confidence as you teach, we will offer sugges-tions about (1) class rules (2) their implementation and (3) discipline. You may want to vary the approach we suggest, but this information will give you a foundation upon which you can build a structure in your own class.

Class Rules

Your class should be a joy for the children. They should walk in and not only feel secure and loved, but also know what is expected of them. To set them up for success, give them rules that are easy to understand and follow. Discuss the rules, have the children repeat them initially, and then repeat them at the beginning of every class period. The way you state the rules depends on the age group you are teaching. If you have young children, use words that they can under-stand, and illustrate the rules on brightly colored poster board with pictures from magazines. Consider the following rules as examples.

1. I will participate in all class activities.
2. When I want to ask a question, I will raise my hand.
3. I will not talk while the teacher is talking.
4. I will listen to the teacher.
5. I will listen and not interrupt when another person in class is answering a question.
6. I will not leave my seat without permission.
7. I will be kind to others in class.
8. When an adult asks me to do something for the class, I will do it without complaining.

If you are creative, going over the rules does not have to be dull and boring. With children age two through seven, you can toss a sponge ball to a child and have him recite one of the rules. Then you can toss the ball to another student and have her recite a rule. Continue until all the rules have been recited. If the students are able, they can toss the ball to each other. As this continues, the children have a great time and learn the rules.

For incentive, you may want to recognize several children who are great examples of following the rules that day. Whatever you decide to do, make it special for the children.

Discipline

> Our fathers disciplined us for a little while as they thought best; but God disciplines us for our good, that we may share in his holiness. No discipline seems pleasant at the time, but painful. Later on, however, it produces a harvest of righteousness and peace for those who have been trained by it. (Hebrews 12:10-11)

We realize that discipline is for our good, and that it can be painful. In a Bible class setting for children, even the most organized and prepared teacher will face some discipline problems. For this reason, we will discuss practical suggestions about how to discipline. These will seem painful at the moment, but will encourage the children in the long run.

The children need to understand from the very beginning that they need to cooperate with you and the other children in the class. You have already explained your plan for the day and discussed the rules. You also need to spell out the plan for discipline if the children are not willing to accept your terms in class. We will discuss step-by-step what we believe is effective.

If a child is blatantly disruptive, disrespectful or unwilling to participate in class, he should be encouraged and helped to settle down, then given a warning to change his attitude. If he will not comply, he should be given a choice to pay attention or to have a "time-out." If he doesn't choose to pay attention, he should be separated from the rest of the class and placed in a corner for time-out. Never be harsh in imposing time-out, but do be firm. The goal is to allow the child to feel a separation from the rest of the group (and the fun). He needs to take responsibility for his actions and be encouraged to change. Guidelines for the amount of time are as follows:

Age	Amount of Time in Time-Out
Two-year-olds	Thirty seconds to a minute
Three- to four-year-olds	Two to three minutes
Five-year-olds and older	Three to five minutes

Look for the first sign of a changed attitude, and warmly encourage the child to rejoin the group. Time-out does its work by (1) causing the child to feel the separation and (2) understanding that his behavior is not acceptable. Time-out should not be used as a threat, and there should be no stigma attached to it.

If a child is shy, chooses not to participate and is not disruptive, or is merely doing the right thing at the wrong time, encouragement is needed to refocus the child. However, this is not cause for time-out.

Time-out should be reserved for rebelliousness, defiance or purposeful disruption of class. If the behavior continues and there is no sign of a change, the child should be taken out of the class and to one of the children's ministry leaders. If the leader cannot convince the child to cooperate with the teacher, then the parents must be asked to come and get the child.

Discuss thoroughly with the parent what has happened, why the child was removed from the class and what will need to happen before he or she can come into the class again.

Make sure to find out from the parents any information about their child that will help you know the best ways to motivate and discipline. For example, a child might have been diagnosed with Attention Deficit Disorder or another condition that will affect behavior in the class. Create a plan with the parent to give structure and guidance so that the child can be set up for success.

Our goal as teachers is to create an environment that is stimulating and fun, yet ordered and instructive. With prayer, planning, preparation—and patience—we can be teachers who inspire our students to know more about God's discipline, guidance, love and acceptance.

20
SAFETY AND LEGAL GUIDELINES

John Bringardner, Esq. • Los Angeles, USA
Clegg & Betty Dyson • Raleigh-Durham, N.C., USA

For we are taking pains to do what is right, not only
in the eyes of the Lord but also in the eyes of men.
2 Corinthians 8:21

Imagine how you would feel if a child under your supervision wandered out of the classroom and fell down a flight of stairs, breaking an arm and losing the vision in one of her eyes. Or what if an adult came to pick up a child after class and convinced you that the mother sent him—and you found out later that the man was an old boyfriend of the mother whose only desire was to hurt her by hurting her child? Or what if a child was sexually abused in your classroom because you were negligent in following the prescribed policies put in place to protect him from just such a damaging occurrence?

All of these are sobering thoughts, to be sure. But these thoughts can easily become reality if we, as children's ministry workers, are not careful and responsible to put into practice the guidelines given to us by godly leaders who seek to protect our children.

General Guidelines

The following general policy guidelines are given by the leadership of the church to be in effect in all churches, whether large or small.

- Always make sure that two adults are with a child (children) at all times—in the classroom, in the hallway, in the restroom, etc.

- Adhere to required ratios of children to adults. (Check with your children's ministry leader to find out the exact ratios required.)

- Carefully set up and monitor check-in and checkout procedures.

- Always keep the door to the classroom open, blocking the bottom portion of the door to keep children from slipping out. (Doors may be closed if they have glass that enables one to see in.)
- Make sure there is no improper physical contact. (See the definitions later in the chapter.)
- Watch for any signs of abuse and molestation. (See the list of signs later in the chapter.)

Screening Guidelines

Children's ministry leaders are given specific instruction as to how to interview and screen each person who desires to serve in the children's ministry. The major requirements are as follows:

- Must have been a baptized disciple for at least six months.
- Must have been a part of the local church for at least six months (if the person has moved from another church).
- Must have no history of having abused a child—even if he or she was involved in only one instance of perpetrating abuse and even if this abuse took place years before he or she became a Christian.
- Must be sure that the person is emotionally prepared to work with children if he or she experienced abuse from someone else.

Complete adherence to these guidelines is imperative. We want to protect our children, our brothers and sisters, and our church. For example:

- If someone accuses a children's ministry worker of abuse, and he was the only worker in the room at the time, he has no proof of his innocence (two-person rule). His reputation would be clouded with no way to remove the cloud.
- If someone takes the church to court because of an allegation of child abuse, the church could end up in a multimillion-dollar lawsuit. If the prosecutor can prove that the ministry was negligent in following up on an applicant's references or in allowing a child to be alone with a worker, he could conceivably win the case even if the accused is totally innocent in the matter.

- Those who have abused in the past could be tempted again. It is unwise to place them in this position of possible temptation.

Signs of Possible Molestation

As a worker in the children's ministry, you should be aware of some of the typical signs of child molestation. The following list is taken from the Youth Ministry Policies for the International Churches of Christ:

Physical signs may include:
- lacerations and bruises
- nightmares
- irritation, pain or injury to the genital area
- difficulty with urination
- discomfort when sitting
- torn or bloody underclothing
- venereal disease

Behavioral signs may include:
- anxiety when approaching church or nursery area
- nervous or hostile behavior toward adults
- sexual self-consciousness
- "acting out" of sexual behavior
- withdrawal from church activities and friends

Verbal signs may include the following statements:
- "I don't like [a particular church worker]."
- "[A church worker] does things to me when we're alone."
- "I don't like to be alone with [a church worker]."
- "[A church worker] fooled around with me."

HIV Considerations

Although medical evidence shows that HIV cannot be passed from one person to another simply by casual contact, we must be very careful to assure both members and visitors that their children are safe from HIV infection. At the same time, we must never discriminate against one of our brothers or sisters who tests positive for the HIV virus.

The church policy states that children's ministry workers who have tested positive for HIV, or who have reason to suspect that they may be HIV positive due to involvement in high-risk activities, cannot volunteer with children five years old and under. This would, of course, include the nursery.

Safety in the Classroom Facility

Sometimes we can take for granted the needs of children when renting a facility for the worship services. Hotels are nice, as are many convention centers, but because of budget limits, some of the spaces we use are not equipped for children's classes. It is important that we make the best of every situation, no matter how difficult it may be.

Safety is a key issue when establishing class space for the children. In the dictionary, the word "safety" is defined as follows: "freedom from danger or risk" or "freedom from injury." As we decide on the class space to be used for the children, it is essential that we establish safety standards. Please pay attention to the following guidelines.

- If the room has no carpeting, it is suggested that you bring rugs to place on the floors. Make sure that the undersides of the rugs have a nonslip surface in order to prevent slipping and sliding. It is important that you use rugs and not blankets, sheets or comforters. The latter slip too easily and can promote injury.

- Cover any unused electrical outlets (especially in rooms for smaller children and the nursery). Use plastic safety covers or electrician's tape to cover open outlets.

- Block any open heaters or radiators so children will not be able to touch them and be burned.

- When fans are used in the warmer months, make sure the fans and cords are out of reach of the children.

- Windows must be closed and locked in winter months. Make sure that the access ways to the windows are blocked so that the children will not be able to get to them. If windows need to be opened, block access to them. It is also important not to use windows that are prone to slam shut and cause injury.

In Case of Fire or Other Emergency

When was the last time you considered an evacuation plan for the children in your class? If you are like most of the teachers in the children's ministry, you probably have not. Well, now is the time to start. With many ministries moving from facility to facility because of availability and growth issues, there must be a plan provided for each location for the safe evacuation of the children in an emergency situation. Please pay close attention to the following guidelines for evacuation in an emergency.

- The children's ministry shall be responsible for formulating a plan for the protection and evacuation of all children and teaching personnel in the event of fire and shall include alternate means of egress (exiting) for all persons involved.

- The children's ministry leader shall make sure that all teaching personnel receive proper instructions on the evacuation procedure specified for the room or area in which they teach. This instruction should take place before new teaching personnel begin their teaching responsibilities.

- When an alarm sounds or the teacher has been notified of an emergency situation, have the children line up in a double line at the door. The assistant teacher and the helpers will escort the children in a quiet and orderly fashion to the nearest designated exit.

- The teacher is the last person to leave the room. Before leaving the room, he or she should close all windows and doors.

- The teacher is responsible for escorting any physically impaired child to the nearest exit and staying with him.

- If any children are in the restrooms during an emergency situation, adults should bring them out and escort them quickly to the nearest exit.

- When exiting the building, walk as far as you can away from the building, but not into the streets. This is a precautionary measure in case fire engines must pass through to get to the building.

- Getting the children out of the building is the first priority! Do not grab diaper bags or toys. If it is cold outside, make sure the children are bundled up in a blanket or adult's coat. Do not try to bring the children's coats.

- If the emergency was a false alarm and the "all clear" is given to enter the building, the teachers will follow the children to the appropriate doors for reentry. When entering the building, the teachers will escort the children back to the classroom in a quiet and orderly fashion.

It is our desire to love our children, and Paul tells us that "love always protects." We should make every effort to protect the little ones who hold such a special place in the heart of Jesus.

Material for this chapter was taken from *Heroes* and from the International Churches of Christ (ICOC) Administrative Policies, with oversight from John Bringardner, Esq. general counsel for the International Churches of Christ.

21
INTERACTING WITH PARENTS

Lois Schmitt • Atlanta, USA

Wanna start a fight? Put twenty Kingdom Kids teachers in a room and ask the following question: "If we could only accomplish one thing in our children's classes, what should it be?" Responses would surely include goals related to Bible knowledge, love of God, training in Bible application, fun at church, strong relationships, love of the kingdom, appreciation of Scripture and spiritual mentors—the list of "most importants" is seemingly endless.

I have also debated this question as I have seen children respond to different class and curriculum philosophies. My conclusion is that what happens *in* the class is far less important than what happens at home *as a result of the class.* A child growing up in the kingdom spends only three to four hours a week at church; he spends the other 164 hours under the guidance of his parents.

Does this let teachers off the hook? Not at all. We have the unique opportunity—and obligation—of communicating with parents what we have observed about their children. We not only teach the children; we equip their parents. The most important accomplishment during a class session may be the observation of a child's character and needs, and the communication of these to his parents.

As Paul wrote, "you yourselves are full of goodness, complete in knowledge and competent to instruct one another" (Romans 15:14). Teachers, especially those who are young or new teachers, frequently underestimate their competence to help parents train their children. It is important to remember that *every* parent, no matter how experienced, needs the input of spiritually minded "outsiders." In Atlanta we have a policy that only lead teachers speak to parents regarding negative class conduct. However, every teacher can be eyes and ears for the lead teacher, and every teacher can communicate encouraging information. Listed below are several practical communication ABCs.

About First Impressions

Communication begins at the registration table. We conducted a Parent/Teacher Communications Survey in Atlanta recently, and parents were very clear about what impressed them at "Check-in."

- Winners: smiles, eye contact, organization, smiles, high energy, neatness, smiles, greeting the children, more smiles.

- Losers: disorganization, craft preparation or food at the registration table, conversations between teachers that are not related to the class, lack of interest in greeting the child, frenzy.

Back to Basics

Little things mean a lot, and hugs get the prize for the simplest way to convey to a child and his parents that he is loved. Hugs can never be overused. They are great for greetings, conversational lags, comfort and hard talks. They are the perfect way to say goodbye, too.

Remembering a child's name is a verbal hug. Few things are as sweet to a parent's ear as the sound of someone saying his child's name, and nothing hurts more than a teacher who does not care enough to know it. If remembering names is not your strong suit, memorize the roll and then use association to remember each name.

Communication Skills

Do not assume that because parents do not ask how their child was, they are not interested—they may just be hurried and distracted. One of the biggest surprises in our communication survey was that parents are hungry for news about *anything* their children do in class: positive, negative or neutral. The fact that a teacher *noticed* and *remembered to tell* them makes the greatest impact on parents. A few scribbled notes jotted down during class can help the memory when it is time for checkout. Positive feedback, of course, is better. My husband had an 80/20 rule when it came to raising our children: share eight encouraging comments for every two corrections. (This is an excellent plan for teachers as well.)

In our nursery we attach small report cards to the diaper bags. Teachers check the appropriate boxes when each baby is changed or fed and note his mood during class as happy, tired, anxious, etc. Parents appreciate this little note.

Any out-of-class communication is also highly valued by parents, maybe because it is unexpected. An encouraging note to a child or his parents is a great way to say, "I love you." A phone call to a child also makes a big impression. When my daughter was in second grade, we got a "How are you?" telephone call from her midweek teacher. That was nineteen years ago, and I *still* remember the teacher's name! One way to facilitate this on a regular basis is to have each teacher in the class "adopt" a few of the children to communicate with. Of course, this is only for friendly and positive communication.

Out-of-class meetings are especially needed when talking with parents about problems not easily solved at checkout. The lead teacher should arrange a mutually convenient time to talk. The midweek or Sunday coordinator should be there as well to help work out a plan for changing the child's behavior.

Discussing Difficult Issues

The letters to the churches in Revelation outline a divine way to correct and counsel: the positive aspects of each church are recognized before problem areas are specifically discussed; Jesus' love and concern are apparent; and vision for future victory is presented.

Of course, in communicating with parents, we must make sure we are "speaking the truth in love" (Ephesians 4:15). Even the toughest disciple is sensitive to issues involving his or her children. Pray for insight and wisdom, and get advice from experienced teachers about how to discuss difficult, emotion-laden areas.

In talking about discipline and character problems, avoid expressing anger or frustration. Honestly, you may need to pray about this beforehand. Be more concerned for the child than the smooth running of the class. His strong points should be appreciated, not merely acknowledged (another chance to apply the 80/20 rule).

Be careful how you describe the child and his behavior. Do not label him as "bad," "hyper," "autistic," "ADD," "ADHD," "bratty" or as a "crybaby." These words have emotional or psychological implications. Be specific and factual without jumping to conclusions. Here is an example of how to and how not to talk with a parent about problematic behavior.

- (Wrong) "Matthew was really hyper today, constantly disrupting the class. Have you had him tested for ADHD?"
- (Right) With child present: "It makes us so happy to have Matthew in our class. However, he had a hard time today sitting still and listening. He could sit for only a few seconds before running around. Have you noticed this?" (Allow parent response.) "Matthew, I know next week you will be my very best listener!" Hug.

Avoid giving negative feedback to visitors, unless they ask specifically for the information.

Expert Counseling

What responsibility does the teacher have to disciple parents, and when should he call for help? The teacher's prime responsibility is to make parents aware of their children's needs, not to disciple the parents. If a parent is receptive, related parenting advice can be given in a relaxed, nonauthoritative way. If the parent is defensive, suggest that he talk with his discipler or regional ministry leader about your observations. Then follow up to see how it went.

The ministry leader should be involved when:

- The parent has resisted advice about talking to his discipler or ministry leader.

- There is reason to believe the child or others would be harmed without timely intervention by the ministry leader.

- The problem affects other disciples or the congregation as a whole.

Teaching gives us the opportunity to touch the lives of the children and their parents as well. We should maintain a positive and faithful attitude and pray for wisdom as we evaluate and communicate.

22
ADAPTATION AND FLEXIBILITY

"Where are we meeting this week?...At the Holiday Inn? I thought we were at the Marshall Middle School....I was in the children's ministry during midweek so I didn't hear the announcement....My voice mail was messed up, so I didn't get any messages this week."

Conversations like these are anything but rare in our worldwide fellowship. We are a moving ministry in many ways: often here one week and there another. This nomadic nature has equipped us to be flexible and adaptable as individuals and as ministries—especially as children's ministries.

This chapter offers input on several areas in which we must be flexible and adapt to the dictates of our environment and to the needs of our children.

1. Teaching the curriculum in unusual situations
   - smaller church with few children
   - all-church or very large group situation
2. Bridging the gap of multilingual communication
3. Including children with special needs

Teaching the Curriculum in Unusual Situations
Amby Murphy• Boston, USA

The Kingdom Kids Curriculum is adaptable to both small and large church settings. In this section we want to make suggestions that will help you think through your particular situation and make decisions that will most help and encourage your kingdom kids.

Smaller Churches with Few Children

You may be in a situation in which you do not have a class of each age group as prescribed in the curriculum. You may have only a few students in each age group and no students in other age groups. You may even be tempted not to teach because you have so few children—

do not give in to this temptation! Even if you have only one child in your children's ministry, make sure that he or she is given loving, prepared instruction and encouragement during the worship service. (But always remember: Even if you have only one child, you still must observe the two-teacher guideline.)

To give input on approaching different types of situations, we will pose several possible scenarios and give some advice about how to approach the structure and teaching in that setting. Hopefully your situation will be addressed in some way through use of these examples.

Always keep in mind that any space chosen for children's classes must be safe. We discourage the use of balconies, stairwells or other potentially dangerous settings. Whatever the space, make sure that it is secure and confined so that children will not get out, hurt or lost.

Example 1
Up to four preschool age children
Up to seven school age children
At least two adults
One "classroom"

The minimum number of adults per class is two. Divide the children according to preschool and school age. If all of the children are preschool age, divide them into two classes: 2s and 3s, and 4s and 5s. Assign one teacher to each class who will be responsible for preparing the preclass and all three activity centers. Preparation for each teacher depends on the age group of the class and whether it is a Core or Supplement Lesson.

Divide your room in half: one side for each class. Create the division with physical barriers if possible. Chairs lined up and covered with colorful, plastic tablecloths make an excellent and appealing barrier. In the case of younger children, consider the safest way to confine the space so that no child can escape easily. Once the room is divided in half, divide each side again into three small areas. Areas can be defined with a small rug, a blanket or tape (if appropriate).

Once you have defined your areas, designate a preclass area. When you are ready to begin the activity centers, bring your whole class to the first center (Bible Story or Life Application) and lead the activity provided for you on the lesson card. Next, lead your group to the area where they will do the second activity center, and finally, lead your class to the area where they will do the third activity center.

If you only have space for one small activity area, then plan a short transition time for the students between activities. For example, after the Bible Story, remove the rug or blanket, have the students stand and stretch and then reorganize them around the work space where they will do their craft. You can define this area with a table and chairs or with a plastic tablecloth on the floor. At the close of that activity, let students once again move or, for younger children, march around briefly. Then regroup for the third and final center activity. If done correctly, children will focus more on "what's next" and less on where they are.

Example 2

　　Up to nine preschool children
　　Up to fourteen school age children
　　At least five adults
　　Two "classrooms"

Divide your children according to preschool and school age. Assign two teachers to the older group in one classroom and three teachers to the younger group in the other classroom. Always put the younger children in the most confined space. Within each classroom, divide the children into two specific age groups and assign one teacher to each group. As in the smaller scenario, the teacher is responsible for preparing the lesson activities for his or her age group. (Note: If all the children in one classroom are in the same class, then the teachers can divide the preparation among them.)

Example 3

　　Ten or more preschool children
　　Fifteen or more school age children
　　Eight or more adults
　　Four or more classrooms

In large settings the teachers can divide the preparation into one activity per center teacher. In this setting, you should have three defined center areas, three designated center teachers and several assistants. The children are divided into three groups, and they rotate to each of the three centers. Each center teacher leads the same activity three times for the three different groups. In these large settings, you may designate teachers for specific centers, i.e. Bible Story teacher, Craft or Game teacher, etc. In this way, the teachers can use and develop their skills as well as provide a consistent environment for the children. Or you may rotate teachers weekly or monthly into different centers, keeping ideas fresh and enthusiasm high, thus training more assistant teachers to rise up to become lead teachers. In either case, the lead teacher, usually the Bible Story teacher, oversees the class to ensure that the centers run smoothly and that the teachers are well prepared.

Large Group Situations

As churches grow, so does the opportunity for church meetings that can number thousands of members and hundreds of children—in one place! Many churches are facing the formidable task of providing safe *and* excellent children's classes in a variety of challenging settings. When the numbers of children are too large to form small groups effectively, then the solution is to run multiple sets of centers. Here is an example from an all-church service in Boston:

At Boston's all-church outdoor service, each children's class averages between seventy-five to two hundred children. There are about two hundred two year olds. This class is divided into Younger Twos (24 to 35 months) and Older Twos (36 to 48 months). The younger class, with about one hundred children, is held under one large tent with a cement floor. The teachers divide the space into three separate sections with secure barriers made from plastic "mesh." Each section's floor is covered with carpets, carpet squares and blankets, and divided into four small activity areas: Bible Story on a blanket, Craft on a table folded on the ground and covered with plastic, Game on a blanket and Snack on a folded table covered with plastic. With twelve adults—four center teachers, four assistants, two bathroom monitors and two supervisors—each section runs four activity centers simultaneously. After children are registered into one of the three sections, they are assigned to an assistant teacher who they will stay with during the entire class period. The assistant teachers lead their groups through the rotation of centers.

The center teachers stay in their areas. The teacher to child ratio never goes above 1 to 3 in this setting. The children have an excellent class and the teachers feel great about the security of the children and their control of the classes.

Regardless of the physical setting in which it is used and regardless of the number of children who are being taught, the goal of the Kingdom Kids Curriculum is to equip disciples with materials that will leave our children with lasting and special memories of their experience in church. As with each new challenge, pray for wisdom and God's guidance to help you plan and implement this program in your church.

Bridging the Gap of Multilingual Communication
Jorge & Debbie Garcia-Bengochea • Miami, USA

If I speak in the tongues of men and of angels, but have not love, I am only a resounding gong or a clanging cymbal. (1 Corinthians 13:1)

Children who come into our classes and do not speak English, or do not speak English as their primary language, often feel apprehensive. They may be confident at home or with friends who speak the same language, but while at church, they are placed in a situation that would be unsettling for anyone. Activities happen around them that they may not understand. Directions are given that they cannot follow. Songs are sung and they do not know the words. They may spend their time in the children's ministry sitting in the back of the class or worrying about what is expected of them. These children have special needs that must be met—or they will leave class feeling discouraged and unloved, and not understanding how special they are to God. With a little planning and consideration, all children can fully participate in learning about God's love and glory.

Identify the Need
Find out what language the child speaks. Get to know the child's family—how are the parents doing? Do they have great relationships in the church, or are they feeling isolated? Are there members in the church who speak the same language? Are they involved with the family? Usually translation of the services is needed in churches located in larger cities where there is significant ethnic diversity.

Accommodate the Child

In most settings you will only have one or two children who really need assistance with English. A simple solution is to have the child sit with children who are bilingual. This way, the child will feel more at ease and can quietly ask questions of his peers. Have a bilingual teacher or a special assistant work next to the child, one who can translate what the teacher says or give direction as needed. Bilingual Bibles are available in many languages and can help the child follow along with the class.

Spend Extra Time in Preparation

Think of ways to encourage children who are learning English, especially if they are new to this country. Talk about the churches in their home countries. Allow them an opportunity to share before the class with the help of a translator. Encourage other children to be friendly and to include them in class activities. Introduce songs and activities that incorporate their languages. Chances are they have music at home and would be glad to bring a sample into class (musical chairs in Spanish?). Explain customs from different parts of the world—and how exciting and big the world that God made is. Our children should feel secure in who they are and where they come from. They need to leave their Kingdom Kids class feeling loved—and love never needs translation.

Including Children with Special Needs
Gail Ewell & Joy Bodzioch • San Francisco, USA

Children's ministry leaders and teachers can partner with parents to ensure that children with special needs of all kinds flourish in the children's ministry. The following points will guide you in choosing adaptations that will help a special-needs child to learn *and to feel included* in class.

Class Selection

Work with parents to decide which class is appropriate for the child. Often, the special-needs child will do fine in a classroom with children of the same chronological age. Be sure to ask questions like,

"What is your child's developmental age? What curriculum age group or grade level would you like for him to learn? What suggestions do you have for helping your child to succeed in the children's ministry?" If necessary, use some or all of the activities from the curriculum for an age group younger than the child. Or if possible, simply adapt the curriculum. Often this can benefit his peers as well. An example would be repeating the memory scripture during the preclass, music, snack and craft times for a special-needs child who needs more repetition in order to learn.

Sensitivity to Needs

Consider the following suggestions that will enable you to meet the individual needs of each child.

- One of the greatest challenges is that special-needs children are more likely to be overwhelmed by crowded classes and loud noises. To address these issues, try decreasing the class size and ensuring that the class routine is well ordered and structured. Be sure that the classroom and bathroom are wheelchair accessible.

- Ask if the child needs extra assistance. Again, work with the parents to decide if another adult volunteer is needed or if a buddy system can be worked out. For example, if the child struggles with auditory learning, a peer could demonstrate how to do activities after the teacher gives verbal instructions.

- Is the child more eager to cooperate if given choices? Asking a child with special needs what song he wants to sing or if he would rather cut or paste at craft time can help him feel more in control.

- Is the child sensitive to certain substances? Some special-needs children are "tactile-defensive." For example, they may be unable to use liquid glue but can use a glue stick. Do they do better when working on colored paper rather than on white or black paper? Are there certain foods they cannot chew or swallow?

- A child who may not excel in other areas may benefit from being given the "honor" of passing out snacks or leading the march to the bathroom. Look for opportunities to give him a leadership role.

- Does the child learn best with visual aids? If so, instructions should be more "show" and less "tell." Memory scriptures and Bible stories can be acted out with play figures, puppets or stuffed animals.

- What resources are available in your congregation? Occupational/physical/speech therapists, psychologists and special education teachers are a great help in designing creative ways to meet the child's needs.

Working with special-needs children can be an exciting challenge. It is an opportunity to become more effective at meeting the unique needs of *every* child in the children's ministry. Depending on the number of special-needs children in your church, you may decide to start one or more classes especially for these children. Contact the San Francisco church for information about starting your own Spiritual Resource Ministry. A manual is also available to guide you through every phase of this process.

We are blessed to be part of a worldwide family, all of whom seek to meet the needs of our kingdom children. Each of us should continue to make every effort (1) to cause our children to feel safe, loved and accepted, and (2) to be willing to adapt in any area in order to better meet their needs.

23
GREAT NURSERIES

Darla Rowe • Nashville, USA

Listen, I tell you a mystery: We will not all sleep, but
we will all be changed.

1 Corinthians 15:51

Whether you have just been asked to work in the nursery, or are in charge of the nursery, you have been given a very special and honored position in God's kingdom: the care and love of his precious babies. To care for the babies in a way that pleases God, we must first provide a safe place for them; second, we must create a loving environment; and third, we must make their time in class fun, while helping them to learn about God at the earliest ages.

A Safe Place

"See that you do not look down on one of these little ones. For I tell you that their angels in heaven always see the face of my Father in heaven." (Matthew 18:10)

"In the same way your Father in heaven is not willing that any of these little ones should be lost." (Matthew 18:14)

- Look closely at the floor before the babies arrive. Any item smaller than the diameter of a quarter is a choking hazard, since everything goes into their mouths. The floor should be clean and free of trash. I have had great nursery teachers who have brought mop and broom to every class to clean a dirty school floor. I have had other great teachers who have brought me handfuls of small objects, including broken glass, from floors of five-star hotels. An electric hand vacuum can be very helpful to ensure that floors are clean and safe.

- Electrical outlet covers must be used on every outlet. A baby can stick fingers or a toy into the outlet. We had a small child pick up a hair pin off the floor and stick it into an electrical outlet under a table that the teachers could not see when they were putting in the outlet covers. The child suffered burns to her fingertips, but, thankfully, did not suffer further harm. An electrician later said that it easily could have killed her. Teachers must get on the floor at children's eye level to see and cover *every* electrical outlet.

- Keep babies away from the door. Keep the door gated at all times. This is inconvenient, especially during check-in and checkout times, but these are the times when you need it most. You never want a baby to slip out the door. There should always be a teacher between the children and the gate. Furthermore, this prevents an adult from being able to bend over the gate and take a baby out without authorization.

- Cushion hard floors with clean rugs (sheets and blankets used alone can cause slipping on uncarpeted floors). Keep children away from walls and furniture with sharp edges.

- Teachers' purses, backpacks, and the like must be placed out of reach of the babies. Many items, such as medications and cosmetics, are very dangerous if ingested by a small child. Also, supply tubs—which may contain plastic trash bags, scissors or other dangerous items—must be kept out of babies' reach.

- Use only toys approved for children less than three years old. Toys should be washed with warm water and soap or bleach, rinsed and dried well between classes. Avoid cloth toys, such as stuffed animals, which are difficult to clean properly.

- Always follow the two-adult rule and the ratio for your age group. For nursery, this is one adult for every two babies. Your nursery might need more adults when you have several fussing babies at the same time.

- Do not allow sick babies or sick teachers into the nursery. You do not want a teacher or baby in the nursery who has had vomiting or diarrhea; or an adult with an abnormal temperature;

or a baby with a temperature of 101 degrees Fahrenheit or higher within the last twenty-four hours. Other possible concerns include: a rash on the upper body, a constant running nose of any color, a persistent cough or extreme fussiness.

- Never give babies any medication at all, even if requested by their parents. Only the parent can administer any medication or perform any medical procedure on their child.

- Be sure that babies have a safe place to sleep. If possible, set up port-a-cribs for sleepers. If you do not have these, use the babies' strollers. If you do not have a stroller, put down a blanket in a corner of the room for the baby to sleep on, away from the playing children.

- Always get the names of the parents and where they will be sitting in case you need to find them during the church service. For larger congregations, you can give the parent a number and flash the number on an electric number board.

- Be sure you only give babies to the correct adult at checkout. Never give a baby to a teen or another child. Have the same adult sign in and sign out for the child—giving you the baby's correct check-in number is not enough. (It helps to have the same nursery teacher at the registration table before and after the service.)

Feeding

Feeding babies is serious business.

- Find out at check-in if there is food or a bottle in the baby's bag. Ask if there is a certain time when the baby needs to be fed. Be sure you know which mothers need to be called to nurse their babies. Write feeding instructions on a removable tag you place on the baby's bag.

- Put the child's name and number on the bag at check-in so that no food or bottles can be confused.

- Never give a baby anything to eat or drink (other than water) that is not provided by the parent, unless the parent has signed his or her approval for that specific snack.

- With babies older than six months, parents can sign approval for a specific snack, such as crackers, dry Cheerios or animal crackers, to be served by the class teachers.
- Be very concerned about possible food allergies or intolerance. (Ask about this at check-in, but with babies, parents may not know this information yet, which is why it can be so dangerous to introduce any new food to a baby.) We had a nursery teacher who gave a fussing baby part of a peanut butter cracker out of her purse. The baby's air passages had begun to close by the time we knew what was wrong: the baby was allergic to peanut butter. God showed us mercy—the children's ministry leader coordinating that service is a pediatrician. But we could have lost a baby that day. Since then any nursery teacher who breaks this policy is no longer a nursery teacher. The stakes are too high.
- Always watch very carefully for choking when babies are having a snack or drinking their bottles.
- It is a good idea to have a nursery teacher who has Infant Heimlich Maneuver/CPR training.

Changing Diapers

Always follow the diaper changing procedures carefully.

- To protect babies from abuse, and to protect nursery teachers from possible accusation, keep diaper changing out in the open, such as on top of a table or changing table or in a designated open space on the floor. Never change a diaper without other nursery teachers close by. When using a tabletop or changing table, always keep one hand on the baby at all times. Never step or look away.
- Ask at check-in if there are special instructions concerning diaper changing. Only apply ointment if it is requested and provided by the parent.
- Wear a clean pair of disposable gloves to change each baby. No baby is to be changed by a teacher who is not wearing disposable gloves. This is a health precaution, as well as a precaution against an accusation of abuse.

- Put something under babies' bottoms, such as paper towels or plastic mats. Change paper towels for each baby. Use babies' own changing mats, or, if you are using the same changing mat for several babies, clean the mat carefully between diaper changes. Be sure that the cleaner is thoroughly wiped off the mat before laying a baby down.

- Put the wet or soiled diaper and used gloves in a plastic bag. Tie the bag and dispose of it properly.

- Wash hands with warm water and soap or antibacterial hand wash after every diaper change.

- It is helpful to have a nursery supply tub with a plastic changing mat (such as children sleep on in kindergarten that folds three ways and fits inside a tub), paper towels, disinfectant spray, disposable gloves, small trash bags, antibacterial hand wash and tissues. You may also want to keep extra wipes and diapers for emergencies.

- Any nursery teacher who changes a diaper in an (undesignated) area of the room not easily visible to other nursery teachers, or who does not wear the disposable gloves provided, should be reported to the children's ministry leader and talked to that day. This has to be taken very seriously for the possible risk she is to the babies and to the church, as well as to herself. If the circumstances were suspicious, the sister may need to be taken out of the children's ministry. If you are convinced the sister was just not thinking, you could talk to her and give her another chance, provided it *never* happens again. If anything like this happens any time in the future, she should either be reassigned to a different role in the children's ministry or, depending on the circumstances, be taken out of the children's ministry altogether.

A Loving Place

He tends his flock like a shepherd:
He gathers the lambs in his arms
and carries them close to his heart;
he gently leads those that have young. (Isaiah 40:11)

This heart, the heart of our Father in heaven, should be the heart of the lead teacher of every nursery class. Then the lead teacher should strive to help each of her nursery teachers to get this same heart.

I want to tell you about the best nursery lead teacher I have ever known, Carolyn Jones, who is the South Region Sunday Nursery One lead teacher most of the time in Nashville. (When she is "off," she is training other nursery teachers or making quilts for the nursery classes.) This is her heart. She really loves the babies and their parents. Peeking into her nursery is a little peek into heaven. Every sister is involved with the babies. The babies are happy because their needs are met and even anticipated. The room is joyful, and unhappy babies are loved and worked with as long as possible before sending for Mommy. I asked her for her secret today because I was working on this chapter (and because I wanted to know). What she shared with me is, I believe, the heart of Isaiah 40:11.

She told me that she does not even try to just give her own love because she knows it is not enough. Instead, her goal is to give the babies and the parents God's love. She prays to love each one just like God loves them. She does not take a baby into her class until she has pulled all of her nursery teachers together and prayed. They get the class roll and pray for every single baby and parent by name. She teaches every nursery teacher to sing spiritual songs to the babies when they are crying. No wonder her class is so wonderful. She calls for God himself to take care of her little ones. And walking by that peaceful room, it is obvious that he does.

Nursery teachers, especially lead teachers and registration teachers, must be warm and loving. Ideally, the lead teacher should be an experienced mom. (Carolyn is an experienced mom and grandmother.) Look for the qualities of warmth, gentleness, joy, wisdom and spiritual maturity in a nursery lead teacher. She must be a woman of strong conviction who will disciple the sisters working in her classroom to be excellent and to follow her example.

Nursery teachers should be women. Most mothers feel better dropping off their baby with another "mommy." Also, this way a nursing mother can come into the nursery to care for her child. When a nursing mother is caring for her child in the nursery, what she observes has a lot to do with how she feels about leaving her child in your nursery.

Reflect carefully on the following questions.

- Is every nursery teacher interacting with the babies (rather than fellowshiping or discipling one another)?

- Are the babies' needs being met? Are all babies obviously being loved and cared for (not just the "easy" or favorite ones)?

- Do the nursery teachers know the babies' names, or do the babies wear name tags so that the teachers call them by name?

- Are the teachers calming to the babies? Is there soft music at appropriate times? Is the playtime fun? Are the songs joyful?

- Are there plenty of age-appropriate toys?

- Do the teachers genuinely seem to want to be there? A mommy knows if you want to be with her precious child.

- Is it obvious that the teachers know the age characteristics of the babies in their class so that their expectations are realistic? (These are listed below in the Age Characteristics section.)

- Does the same nursery teacher feed, change and care for the same babies each week so that the baby knows the nursery teacher and the nursery teacher knows the baby?

- Are aggressive babies worked with so that no babies are harmed? (We will discuss appropriate ways to deal with this later.)

- Is the lead teacher gentle and encouraging to parents who need help with leaving their children or who have a lot of questions?

- Does the lead teacher help the parents when babies are having a difficult time, such as not wanting to be left in class, being aggressive or biting? (We will talk more about this later.)

A Learning Place

> From the lips of children and infants
> you have ordained praise. (Psalm 8:2)

Use a class schedule. Here is an example. (For an explanation of the italicized words, please see paragraphs below.)

Time	Activity
9:30-10:15	Check-in; babies on blankets with *Play Toys*; cassette tape of music playing ("Wee Sing Bible Songs," etc.)
10:15-10:30	*Group Singing*
10:30-10:45	*Group One* has *Cradle Roll Lesson* at table (the length of the lesson should be determined by the age and attention span of the group—fifteen to twenty minutes) *Group Two* has *Center Toys* on floor with feeding and changing diapers as needed
10:45-11:00	Trade *Group One* and *Group Two*
11:00-11:30	Check to make sure all babies have been fed and changed; bags prepared for checkout

What is the difference between Play Toys and Center Toys?

Center Toys are toys that the teachers will use to interact with the babies. They need to be age appropriate for the babies in your nursery. Examples of Center Toys are cardboard or plastic books, large plastic balls to roll, plastic stacking rings, the most simple four-piece plastic or wooden puzzle (one piece in one opening, preferably with a knob handle), plastic baby dolls, baby trains or cars, baby blocks, busy box, noisemaking baby toys.

Play Toys can be these same types of toys or other age-appropriate baby toys. The reason to have both a Play Toys tub and a Center Toys tub is to give the babies variety during the class.

Garage sales, consignment shops, dollar stores and parental donations are great, money-saving ways to improve the quality and quantity of your toys. Ask nursery parents if they would like to help by donating one of their baby's toys. The babies enjoy having a familiar toy at Bible Class. Let families of older children know you would love to have their no-longer-used baby toys.

How do you have a great Group Singing time? Move visuals around as you sing so that all babies can see visuals well. Sing baby songs and Bible songs that are fun and happy.

How do you have a great Group Singing time?

A very important part of any nursery class is music and songs. Make the music and the singing in your class the best you can make it. Use colorful props; lead with enthusiasm; have all teachers singing and helping babies participate; move very quickly from one song to the next.

For Group Singing, put away Play Toys, as you sing the "Clean Up Song." Sit on a blanket together with teachers holding babies. The teacher leading the group stands up, leading singing and holding up visuals.

It is okay to sing "The Itsy Bitsy Spider," "Old MacDonald" and other children's favorites at times. You can make them spiritual by, after singing about an animal, stopping and saying, "Who made the cow? God did." Remember that this is the children's ministry and not day care. Therefore, use every opportunity to make the class spiritual, while keeping it fun and age appropriate for the babies. It is fine to hum "Sanctuary" to a baby you are helping to fall asleep, but these types of songs will not keep the attention of a group of young children.

You can also use a familiar tune when going from one activity to another by changing the words of the song to whatever you are doing. For example, to the tune of "Farmer in the Dell" you can sing, "It's time to get our seat. It's time to get our seat. It's time to start our Bible Class. It's time to get our seat." Or "It's time to eat our snack. It's time to eat our snack. Because this baby is hungry, it is time to eat our snack." Often babies get fussy during transition times in the class, and singing can really help them feel secure. Singing the same song between activities each week helps them to know what is coming, which helps them to transition better to the new activity.

What is a Cradle Roll Lesson for babies?

Do you know that the babies in your nursery class are learning at the fastest rate that they will ever learn in their lives? What a great time to start teaching them that God made them and loves them. Do not fall into the baby-sitting mind-set of nursery. Kingdom Kids nursery is much more than baby-sitting.

How do you get babies to sit for the Cradle Roll Lesson?

Use baby seats that attach to a table so that one group of babies at a time can sit at the table for the lesson. The teacher sits in a chair in the middle of one of the long sides of a rectangular-shaped table with a baby at each end of the table and three babies on the long side of the table facing her. If there are seven babies, she attaches one on either side of her as well. Other tables, such as kidney-shaped tables or round tables work well.

The table has to be strong enough so that the chairs with babies in them will not tip the table over. A table with a ledge close to the edge of the table (underneath the table) will not work if it keeps the baby seat from attaching firmly to the table. Experiment by attaching the baby seat and pressing down on the baby seat to see if the seat stays firmly attached to the table and to make sure the table does not tip over. Another way to get babies to sit for class is to pull up strollers in a semicircle with children sitting in the strollers.

A third way is to have several teachers hold children sitting in a semicircle. (This is not as good because it is hard for teachers to hold two to three babies at a time.)

How many children have the Cradle Roll Lesson at a time?

You cannot do the lesson effectively for a large group all at once. The babies need to be "up close and personal" with the lesson props and the teacher doing the lesson. In a large group, they are easily distracted and will start to "wander." Four to seven children is a good number in one group. If you have eight to fourteen children in your nursery, do the lesson twice—once for each group. If you have fifteen to twenty-one children in your nursery, do the lesson three times.

You will need enough baby seats or strollers or laps (or combination of strollers and laps) for the children in one group. Be sure to buckle babies into seats or strollers.

What is the best age grouping and class size for nursery classes? What are the possible class breakdowns?

You can break your nursery-age babies into three separate classes. Nursery One is for the youngest babies. Nursery Two can be for babies who are walking, and the Toddler class is for babies who are eighteen or nineteen months to those just turning two.

Putting a baby into Nursery One depends on several factors. They need to be old enough to be in a group of other babies, not requiring constant one-on-one care and they need to be able to enjoy the class. The age may vary from church to church depending on the number of classrooms and the number of teachers available. In some churches babies are taken at three to four months. In others babies are taken at six months. Obviously, younger babies require more one-on-one attention. The two to one ratio works well for babies six months and older. Younger babies may need extra teachers.

When babies are walking well, it is good to have a Nursery Two. If you have a lot of babies in your Nursery Two, you can have a Toddler class for babies who are from eighteen or nineteen months to babies who have just turned two. We have found that children do great being moved up to the two-year-old class when they are twenty-seven months. They are more able to sit in the Learning Centers and do the activities successfully at this age than at twenty-four months.

Ideally a five-hundred square-foot room accommodates up to fifteen babies and their teachers (with some space for nursing mothers). Classroom size will vary from church to church, based on the number of babies and the space available.

What if you have a huge nursery?

If you are in a situation where you have a very large nursery (more than twenty-one babies), divide the room so that teachers and children are in two or four separate groups, with no more than fifteen babies in each group and a teacher in charge of each group. The teacher teaching the lesson can go to each group and do the lesson with that group of babies and teachers, with teachers holding babies.

The groups of children not having the lesson can play on the floor with their Center Toys. If there are two groups of babies, use one set of toys for each group at the beginning of class. Put toys in tubs. Then do Group Singing with the whole room together (but keep the babies in their groups). Have a set of props for Group Singing for each group. Then switch toy tubs so that each group of babies now has the other set of toys to play with during Center Time. If there are four groups, each set of two groups can switch toys. It is important to divide up a large nursery this way so that every baby is carefully watched and cared for in a smaller group. This also helps a huge nursery not be as wild.

How is a Toddler Class different from a Nursery One or Nursery Two Class?

Using the sample schedule suggested above for Nursery One and Two, a Toddler class would be the same until 10:30. After Group Singing, the children would be divided into three groups. One group would have their Toddler Cradle Roll Lesson in one corner of the room on the floor. The second group would have their Center Toys and Books Center in a second area of the room, while their diapers were being checked. The third group would sit at the table for Snack/Craft Center (using the same hook-on chairs discussed above) for a simple snack, such as animal crackers and water, followed by a very simple craft.

The toddler teachers would then help to rotate the three groups of children through each center.

After all children have completed all centers, children sit on a blanket with teachers. A teacher plays music on cassette tape for singing and dancing. The teacher gives baby-safe musical instruments to the children for playing along with the music and blows bubbles for the children.

Age Characteristics

This section will give the characteristics for babies at different ages so nursery teachers will know their babies and have realistic expectations of what they can do at certain ages. Keep in mind, however, that every baby develops in his or her own unique time frame, not according to any schedule or list.

At four to six months, baby can:
- Explore the world with hands and eyes
- Reach out for an object
- Smile, coo and expect a response

At six to twelve months, baby can:
- Sit alone
- Learn to move through space—scoot, creep, crawl, walk
- Notice small details
- Show anxiety in new situations
- Miss mom or dad
- Respond to his or her own name
- Drink from a cup
- Find a covered object
- Point to objects
- Understand some words ("Mommy," "bottle," "no," etc.)
- Imitate banging, clapping, waving

At twelve to nineteen months, baby can:
- Say some words (three or four at one year)
- Build a tower of two blocks
- "Jabber" with expression
- Listen to rhymes, finger plays and jingles for three to four minutes
- Show affection
- Stack rings on a spindle
- Walk alone
- Sit down from a standing position
- Understand a lot of words (though he or she cannot say them yet)

At eighteen to twenty-four months, baby can:
- Climb
- Build a tower of three or four blocks
- "Scribble" in a circular motion
- Refer to herself by name
- Follow a one-step direction
- Name some objects
- Point to his own body parts
- Do it "myself"
- Say "no"
- Work a simple inlay puzzle (one piece per hole)
- Fill and dump
- Imitate adults

Challenging Situations

Babies Who Cry

With young babies who will not stop crying, try everything you can think of (food, bottle, check diaper, walk, rock, sing, pacifier, "blankie"). Before you get the parent, there is one last thing that sometimes works: give the baby to a different person. Sometimes being with a new person helps the baby to settle down. But if nothing helps, send for the parent.

With older babies (six months or older) who don't stop crying, they may be "clingers." Clingers want their mommy, and nobody else will do. (By the way, the following plan works well with young children, too.)

If the baby is new in your class, do the best you can (same as above) for as long as you can, but you may eventually have to send for the parent.

The parent can sit in the class a time or two to let the child adjust to the new class to see if that will help. The parent can then try to leave, and see how the child does.

If that does not work, and if the child comes to class regularly, the lead teacher and the parent together will make a plan.

"The Plan" is that the first class period the parent will leave the child in the class for fifteen minutes. (The parent needs to leave the class quickly with no hanging around.) No matter how much the child screams, the child stays in class for fifteen minutes. Then the parent comes and picks up the child (without being sent for).

The next class period, the parent comes back after sixteen minutes; the next class period, seventeen minutes; the next class period, eighteen minutes; and so on.

When the parent comes to pick up the child, the parent first stands outside the door and listens (where the child cannot see the parent). If, by chance, the child is not crying, the parent leaves for a few minutes; then comes back and checks again, etc.

Even though this is inconvenient for the parent, the parent should not "shame" the child or be negative, etc. The parent should just get the child like they would if class were over. It should be matter-of-fact. The parent should not, however, make it too much fun either. (No coke or snack machine trip. Sit down in the rear of the service or in a chair in the hall.)

With an older baby or young child, the parent should pray with the child every night for God to help the child to love Bible Class. The parent needs to be excited on the way to Bible Class. Sing Bible Class songs in the car.

In this way the child is "weaned" from the parent. The child always knows the parent is coming, and the child also learns that crying and screaming will not manipulate the teacher and parent into giving the child his or her way.

The first time the child stays all the way through class happily is a big day. The child has learned a valuable lesson in character. Suggest the family go for ice cream or to the park to celebrate their child's victory.

The secret to the success of this plan is consistency. It will not work if the child does not come to class regularly. It must be used both on Sunday and midweek. If the child is sick and misses a couple of class periods, the plan may need to be started over again if the child will not stop crying the first class period the child comes back to class.

Babies Who Are Aggressive

Aggressive babies may hit, scratch or bite. They may kick or throw objects at other people. These babies are sometimes imitating behavior they have seen from older siblings or from other children at day care. Sometimes these children are from violent or otherwise unhappy homes in which someone is often angry with them or older siblings pick on them or tease them. Sometimes they are simply frustrated because they want something they can't get or because they cannot communicate with words yet. Sometimes a child can be aggressive as a physical symptom of a physical, mental or emotional disorder.

When young children are aggressive, do not immediately jump to the worst conclusions about their home life—but don't shrug it off either. The children's ministry leader should be notified if a child is consistently aggressive. The children's ministry leader may want to sit down with the parent and the lead teacher to talk about the child and how to help. If there is a professional caregiver or teacher or special education teacher in your church, you may want to have them observe the child and give input if this is helpful to the situation.

Once you know a child is aggressive, assign him a "bodyguard." This is a nursery teacher who stays with the child at all times to protect the other children. This teacher should be firm when the child is aggressive, but the teacher should love the child and never be harsh or lose her temper with the child. The two wings of the airplane to help this child to change are unconditional love for the child and a brick wall when it comes to hurting another person. (This must include not hurting adults. They need to learn that it's not okay to be aggressive with parents or teachers either.)

The nursery teacher must train the child with encouraging words when the child is making good choices (not being aggressive, being kind, etc.). The teacher must train the child with directional words when the child is starting to be aggressive. "No, you may not hit Sarah. Let's get this toy," helping the child to go in a different direction. The teacher must intervene so that the child is not successful in being aggressive.

The teacher must help the child to be successful in other ways. "You built a great tower." Give the child as much praise as possible. Give the child good ways to have plenty of physical movement. "Do you want to knock down the tower? Yaah! You knocked it down. Do you want to build it again?"

If the child hurts another child, there must be a consequence. The nursery teacher in charge of the child is the one who should give the consequence under the oversight of the lead teacher. (Discipline is ineffective without relationship.)

The consequence should be age appropriate. You can take the child away from the other children to a corner of the room. If he will sit alone, you can tell him he needs to "think about being kind to his friends," and leave him there for two to three minutes, depending on his age. If he will not sit, sit down with him, saying the same thing. After the time is up, ask him if he is ready to be kind to his friends. If he is not cooperative, sit for a couple more minutes saying the same thing. Go back into the group with him, watching him carefully to make sure he is not going to take it out on another child if he still has any anger. Try to help him to "be happy" or "be sweet" before rejoining the group if possible. If he is old enough, help him to say "I'm sorry" to the child he hurt.

If this does not change the behavior, call the parent. Go over what you are doing in class, and encourage the parent to do the same at home. Have the parent take the child out of class. Try again next class period. The child must have the same type of care on Sundays and midweeks in order to bring about change. Again, consistency is the key.

Babies Who Bite

Children who bite are handled the same way as aggressive children are. (See the section above.) However, biting can be very dangerous to the child being bitten. Pediatricians suggest that someone sustaining a human bite wound that breaks the skin should seek medical attention in case antibiotics are needed. For this reason, nursery teachers must do everything in their power to keep a biter from biting another child.

Once you know a child is a biter, the child needs to have a "bodyguard" who watches that child every moment until he has not attempted to bite (anywhere—school, home, etc.) for some time.

If a child bites another child, call for the parent to remove the child from class that day (and encourage the parent to discipline the child). Start again next class. Handle the child the same on Sundays and midweeks. Be very consistent. Help the parent to handle the child the same at home as you are at church. (Biting cannot be considered as "playing" or funny anywhere, or it will be confusing to the child.)

With children who like something in their mouths to chew on, or who may be cutting teeth, be sure they always have something appropriate in their mouths at all times, so they will not be tempted to bite another person.

For a child who has been bitten, immediately clean the wound with soap and warm water. Cover it with a Band-Aid if needed. Call for the parent if the bite mark is more than a superficial wound.

If you do not need to call for the parent, when the parent comes to pick up the child after class, the lead teacher should point out the bite mark to the parent. Apologize profusely. Explain that you now have a plan in place to help the other child not to bite any more and that you will do everything you can to ensure that this does not happen again. The lead teacher then needs to give a written report of the biting incident to the children's ministry leader.

Once a biter has bitten Sarah, never allow the biter an opportunity to bite Sarah again. For some reason, biters often go to the same child in the class again and again to bite. You must make sure that this does not happen.

Children older than two who bite should stay out of class until the parent is certain that the child has not attempted to bite for some time. The reason for this is that they could hurt a younger or smaller child very badly. (The older the child, the longer he stays out of class. We had a kindergartner stay out for a month.) Do your best to assist the parent in putting into practice the advice given here on working with aggressive and biting children. These children need the two wings of the airplane—unconditional love and prevention from doing harm at home—as well.

"A [great nursery teacher] who can find? She is worth far more than rubies" (Proverbs 31:10). A nursery teacher who gives her heart first to God, and then wholeheartedly to the babies in her care, is truly a jewel in God's kingdom.

Never underestimate the impact you are having on every parent who knows that her child is loved in your nursery. Never underestimate the power you have as you help to raise up the next generation of disciples. The God of the universe sees every tear you wipe and every need you meet. He sees every safety precaution you take. And as you do these things, remember that you are doing them for Jesus himself, as if he were a baby again here on earth in your nursery (Matthew 25:37-40). This is how he feels about every child in your care!

I would like to thank the late Barbara Lloyd for giving me a heart for the babies. She is alive in all I have shared with you.

24
UNDERSTANDING PRESCHOOLERS

Katie LaBombard • Boston, USA

Effective teaching requires that you have both a solid grasp of the material you are teaching and a good understanding of those you are teaching it to. A second grader will process what he or she experiences very differently from a preteen, and four-year-olds are not able to learn from a lesson if it is modeled after a Bible discussion for adults. While the Kingdom Kids Curriculum has been designed with issues of child development and age-appropriateness in mind, it is crucial for you, the teacher, to know as much as possible about the age group you are working with and to be familiar with the lessons you will be teaching to them.

2s and 3s

Children in the 2s and 3s class are at one of the most exhilarating stages of their lives—a time of discovering their independence. They experience great excitement as they learn to accomplish things on their own. "I want to do it!" is a frequent cry from a child of this age, as both the child and the adult become accustomed to this newfound independence. In fact, it is this very independence that has given this age group the affectionate name of the "terrible twos."

During this stage of development, children tend to have a language of their own. They do or say things that we might need a translator to understand! The more you understand them, the easier it is to communicate with them.

4s and 5s

As children enter this stage of life, they become more intellectually curious. They are learning how to write and read, and they are beginning to understand the concept of numbers: counting, adding and subtracting. While four- and five-year-olds love to sit, listen and learn, they are not able to stay at one task for very long. It is important to vary activities to keep their interest.

There can be a large developmental gap between a four-year-old and a five-year-old. A child of four will not be able to do the same things that a five-year-old can do, and they may become frustrated from trying. At the same time, a child of five may finish an activity quickly and become bored while waiting for others to finish. It is important to be conscious of time during an activity. You may need to help the four-year-olds by doing some of the more difficult steps with them, thus helping all the children to feel successful.

Offer Choices

Choices are an important key to communicating with a preschooler. This means allowing choices during the Preclass and Post-class activities, having a variety of materials available for the children to choose from. But it also means allowing choices for right behavior. Because of their desire for independence, preschoolers will often find themselves in conflict with adults. When redirecting them, it is important to give two possibilities: one being what the child should do and the other being either a consequence of the wrong action or a way for the adult to help. For example, if a child of two or three holds a toy, it automatically becomes his possession in his own mind. If the toy does not truly belong to him and you try to take it from him, the child may scream at you or hit you. Although this behavior is typical, it is not to be accepted. At this time it is helpful to give the child a choice. "It is time to share now. Either you can give Matthew the toy or I can give it to him. Which do you choose?" After the child chooses, give him a gentle reminder to always share toys. And always be sure to praise a child for making the right choice.

Giving children choices helps them not only to be independent, but also to take responsibility for their actions. It helps a classroom run smoothly as you and the children work together to resolve conflict. There is far less struggle for power and control—something that the child clearly wants, but that you need to possess and maintain.

Other Pointers

Speak to children on their level physically. Most adults are a great deal taller than preschoolers are. This can be very intimidating to small children. Sit, bend down or kneel when addressing them.

- Speak in short, concise sentences, using language that the child will understand. This is especially important when you are giving directions. It is often best to give one direction at a time. For example, when making a craft say: "First put the glue on the paper. Good. Now, put the cotton on the glue."

- Speak positively. You will get much better responses from the children. For instance, if a young child is running, say to him, "Use walking feet" instead of saying, "No running." This creates a much more positive atmosphere with less frustration on the part of the children and the teachers.

- Give choices when disciplining a child. For example, say: "You have a choice: You can sit with us and listen, or you can go sit in a 'time-out.' Which do you choose?" As discussed earlier, this allows children to take responsibility for their actions and will help them make the right choice.

- Wear nice looking, comfortable clothes. This will keep you from looking stiff and formal. It causes the parents (and the children) to feel that you are ready for interactive teaching, which involves a lot of movement. On the other hand, it also says that the children are important enough for you to dress nicely when teaching them.

- Spend lots of time sitting on the floor and playing with the children. This will help you not only to keep order, but to gain the respect of the children as well. Playing with them on their level shows them that they are valuable to you.

Eager Sponges

It is important for you to understand that although preschool children are very young, they are quite capable of learning. In fact, they are very much like sponges, eagerly soaking up all that they can. Understanding their stage of development will help you to satisfy their desire for learning. Inappropriate expectations, whether too high or too low, will hinder you from "connecting" with the children, and valuable opportunities for helping them to know God will be lost. Become a student of your students, and you will then be able to discern how to teach in such a way that they will benefit the most from your time together.

Understanding the Preschool Lesson

The *Seeds of Faith* lessons have been carefully designed for preschoolers. Young children need lots of repetition to help them learn, especially 2s and 3s. The more repetition that children have, the more they will remember the Biblical principles being taught.

Curriculum Goals

The following diagram represents the cumulative unit goals for the preschool cycle of curriculum. It is the backbone of the scope and sequence and provides the foundation on which each consecutive cycle will be built and integrated. Every lesson contains at least one specific focus from the list below, in addition to a scripture reference (or Bible truth for 2s and 3s), a memory verse (4s and 5s only) and a life application.

Curriculum Goals	Application to Preschoolers
Bible Knowledge	**THEME:** The Bible is God's word. **CHARACTERS:** Adam and Eve, Noah, Moses, David, Jesus, Joseph and Mary **EVENTS:** Creation, Birth of Jesus, Miracles of Nature, Paul and the Early Church
Love for God	**CONCEPTS:** God is giving; God takes care of me; God loves me.
Relationships	**FAMILY:** Obey parents; purpose of family is to serve God. **CHURCH:** Obey teachers; be thankful for the church. **WORLD:** Bring friends to church; give to others.
Character of Christ	**CHARACTERISTICS:** Jesus loves me; Jesus obeyed God and his parents; Jesus was happy and thankful.
Prepared to Answer	**CONCEPT:** God gave us the Bible.

With these goals in mind, the curriculum is divided into thematic units, each containing up to eight lessons. Each preschool lesson contains a Preclass activity and three activity centers: Bible Story, Life Application and Craft. Within a unit there may be a Bible Story or Life Application activity that is repeated in several lessons. Listed below is a description of each activity and its frequency of repetition within a unit.

Activity Centers

Preclass Activity

The Preclass Activity is designed to prepare the children for the lesson that will follow. Usually a start-up activity held prior to the formal class time, it can be either an individual or small group project.

Lessons for the 2s and 3s have "Preclass centers." These centers are groups of activities that remain virtually the same from lesson to lesson and unit to unit. Each time the unit changes, materials within the centers are replaced with those which best reflect the theme of the new unit.

Lessons for 4s and 5s each have a unique Preclass Activity. Many times this activity will be used to make something that will be needed later on in the lesson, such as a prop in the Bible Story. It is also recommended that two other activities, such as blocks and puzzles, be made available to allow the children a choice during this time.

Bible Story

In this center the Bible Story is presented in a way that is both meaningful and engaging to the child. This center is the pivotal portion of each lesson. Each of the other centers have activities that in some way reflect the lesson theme taught in the Bible Story center.

For the 2s and 3s, this is the most repetitious center in the unit. There are two Bible Stories in each unit. These are repeated four times within two lessons (twice in the Core and twice in the Supplement). Each Bible Story that occurs within a lesson for 4s and 5s is unique. Feel free to bring this center to life with extra props and lots of dramatization!

Life Application

The lesson theme is reinforced in this center with an emphasis on applying it to life. The primary activity is usually a game, role play or a story. All lessons along with the primary activity also feature a Scripture Memory activity to help children remember important Bible truths (simple statements based on a scripture) for the 2s and 3s and Bible verses for the 4s and 5s.

Each lesson has a unique Life Application activity that is repeated in subsequent lessons for emphasis.

Craft

Crafts have often been described as the way that children "take notes." In this center the children will make a craft that reinforces the lesson theme and provides them with a meaningful reminder of the story. In each lesson, both the Core and Supplement have a unique craft.

Teaching preschoolers is exciting and challenging—but ultimately rewarding. You are laying the foundation for many years of Biblical teaching to follow. Remember to enjoy your time with this unique age group!

25
UNDERSTANDING FIRST AND SECOND GRADERS

Amby Murphy • Boston, USA

In the motion picture *Pooh's Grand Adventure: The Search for Christopher Robin*, Christopher Robin is faced with a painful reality—tomorrow is his first day of school, and he shall not be able to meet Pooh at their special place under the tree in the hundred-acre wood. They promise each other that they will be friends forever—even when they are apart. And the adventure begins.

Who Are They?

Life for first graders is a grand adventure. School is shaping their world. Fun and play have a new twist—order. Letters become words; pictures tell stories; faces and shapes have patterns, and colors make other colors. Their minds are overflowing with new ideas and what to do with them. The key to remember is *order.*

Those in second grade then become masters of order. They read and write with more confidence. They have a new adventure—relationships! They identify, compare, contrast and associate. The order of first grade is now their key to unlocking new and more challenging patterns and puzzles. Not only are they learning relationships of letters and numbers, they are also learning to build their own relationships and make friends. The key to remember is *relationships.*

Who Is God?

To most first graders, God is good. God is a loving Father. He is strong; he is always right, and he knows everything. He is Jesus' Father and he loves children. God wrote the Bible and he wants children to obey what it says. God loves to hear them pray. God wants them to obey their parents. God wants everyone to be happy. God is happy when we obey and he is not happy when we do not. Children this age have a firm faith in the goodness of God and are beginning to think about him in relation to themselves. The key to remember is *God is good.*

To the second grader whose identity is beginning to be shaped more by friends and others' opinions, God is also becoming relational. They think more in terms of cause and effect and may begin to question God. Children this age are sensitive to what others think and also to what God thinks of them. They are eager to please. They may be quick to feel as though they have failed and will need lots of encouragement. They need to be reassured of God's love for them. The key to remember is *God loves me*.

Who Are You?

You are a teacher, a role model, a friend and a living example of Jesus. Children will see you first as their teacher as you feed their hungry minds and hearts with exciting new ideas and adventures. Do not be concerned if you are not a teacher by profession, for your real "profession" is Christ, and this is all they need. For children who come from homes where one parent is not a disciple, you are an adult role model. How you treat them and others will be the Bible coming to life in ways that they *may not see anywhere else*. For those struggling with adult relationships in school or in the community, you are a friend. And above all, you are Jesus to each of them as you strive to help them see God in ways they will never forget. The key to remember is: *Be like Jesus*.

What to Remember

Fun-loving is my nature; it's really quite true!
I've got such imagination. I'll share it with you.
Responsibility is something I need you to teach me.
Singing is fun, and I'll try hard if you lead me.
Teacher, I'll give you all that I've got.
     If you do the same, then we'll learn a lot!

Since I'm older and wiser, you'll see what I mean.
Eager to please; I'm a speed machine!
Channel my energy; I need self-control.
Only please be gentle or to despair I may fall.
Never, oh never, give up on your part.
Develop in me a love-for-God heart!

First and Second Grade Lesson

Curriculum Goals

The following diagram represents the cumulative unit goals for the First and Second Grade cycle of curriculum. It builds and reinforces concepts learned in the previous cycles. Every lesson contains *at least* one specific focus from the list below, in addition to a scripture reference, a memory verse and a life application.

Curriculum Goals	Application to First and Second Graders
Bible Knowledge	***THEME:*** The Bible is God's Word; God chose special men to write the Bible; the Bible is to be obeyed. There is a relationship between Old and New Testaments; major divisions of the Bible are the Law and Prophets and Jesus and Apostles. ***CHARACTERS:*** Adam and Eve, Cain and Abel, Noah, Abraham and Sarah, Isaac and Jacob, Moses, Joshua, Joseph, David, Saul, Solomon, Esther, Samson, Gideon, Deborah, Samuel, Daniel, Jeremiah, Ezekiel, Elijah, Jesus, Joseph and Mary, Peter, James and John, Paul, Andrew, Thomas, Judas, Ethiopian Eunuch. ***EVENTS:*** Creation, Flood, Exodus, Ten Commandments, Wanderings, Birth of Jesus, Temptation of Jesus, Miracles of Nature, Miracles of Healing, Jesus' Crucifixion and Jesus' Resurrection, Paul and the Early Church, the Church Grows, Pentecost, Cornelius, Eternal Life.
Love for God	***CONCEPTS:*** God is giving; God takes care of me; God loves me; God made me; God knows all about me; God is not happy when I do wrong; God is happy when I do right; God is our Father; God is powerful; God is patient and kind; God is not easily angered; God has a plan for me; God is always good; I am special and unique to God.
Character of Christ	***CHARACTERISTICS:*** Jesus loves me; Jesus obeyed God and his parents; Jesus was happy and thankful; Jesus' purpose was to serve and to save; Jesus did his best; he loved all people. Jesus was honest, joyful, forgiving and had self-control.

Character of Christ *(continued)*	*VALUES:* Pleasing God versus pleasing people; judging people by their hearts and not by their appearances; the value of people versus possessions.
Prepared to Answer	*CONCEPT:* God gave us the Bible; the Bible teaches us right from wrong, good from bad, what makes us happy and sad. *MORALITY:* God made us special as a boy or a girl; as disciples we are different from the world. *RELEVANCY OF THE BIBLE:* Not everyone follows the Bible or believes it; not everyone follows all of the Bible. Spiritual responses to violence, drugs, immorality, and the media.
Relationships	*FAMILY:* Obey parents; purpose of family is to serve God; serving and helping in the home; personal responsibility; obeying the first time. *CHURCH:* Obey teachers; be thankful for the church. *WORLD:* Bring friends to church; give to others; understand world missions. *UNIVERSALS:* Respect, openness, sharing, cooperation, loving others, listening, forgiveness, resolving conflict, responsibility, gratitude.

The third and final cycle of the Kingdom Kids primary curriculum, *Seeds of Faith,* is First and Second Grade. This cycle features two new activity centers: Scripture Memory and Bible Skills. These lessons are designed to transition first and second graders from the "fun and games" of preschool and kindergarten into a more skills-oriented approach. Children are sure to enjoy these activities as they develop their abilities to memorize scripture, to recognize key words and to order books of the Bible, as well as to pray with others, to talk about their feelings and to apply Scripture to their lives.

Activity Centers

Every week, children will participate in six different learning centers: three in the Core Lesson and three in the Supplement.
- Core: Bible Story
- Core: Craft
- Core: Scripture Memory
- Supplement: Life Application

- Supplement: Game
- Supplement: Bible Skills

Bible Story and Life Application

Children will participate in a weekly Bible Story that is fun and relevant to their lives as they master key words and concepts. In the Supplement lesson, the Bible Story is reviewed and applied in the Life Application center. This activity looks at the Bible Story from a personal perspective and helps children to make real-life applications. Both the Bible Story and Life Application lessons are scripted to help ensure that each lesson has age-appropriate language and concepts. Anyone who is prepared can lead an exciting and life-changing class.

Craft

Always a favorite, the craft is a tangible memory of the child's Bible Story experience. Children will make crafts that they can share with others at home and at school. With step-by-step instructions and diagrams, the teacher is set up for success. You do not have to be an art teacher to help the children to make a great craft—you just have to be prepared.

Scripture Memory

The Scripture Memory center is new and will help children learn and memorize Scripture through games and fun activities. Not only will they learn precious truths from God's word, but the children will build friendships as they work and play together. Inspired by techniques used by language teachers, this center is designed to help lay a foundation of scripture memory that will last a lifetime.

Game

From musical chairs to fun with blindfolds, children are sure to have a great time playing games that reinforce key concepts and that review Bible knowledge. Friendships continue to be deepened though teamwork and healthy competition.

Bible Skills

Based on target academic skills, this new center uses basic reading, writing, ordering and identification to help children get to know their way around the Bible. Ultimately, this activity center has been designed to prepare children for the challenges of more intensive Bible skills in the next cycle, *Generation: Next.*

What's Next?

Children who successfully complete this two-year cycle will be familiar with the books and general significance of the Old and New Testament. They will have memorized about one hundred scriptures and begun to master skills such as locating Bible verses and using a concordance. These children will not only have vivid memories of Bible stories, but they will also have discussed, prayed about and experienced personal applications of many Bible passages. Ultimately, the children who complete this cycle will be ready to enter the Third and Fourth Grade class, *Generation: Next,* to begin a comprehensive survey of Bible history, events and personalities.

26
UNDERSTANDING THIRD AND FOURTH GRADERS

Amby Murphy • Boston, USA

Stop and think about what you remember from third and fourth grades. School? Friends? Choices? Today's students face pressures that most of us never dreamed of at this young age. Will your class be a safe haven for their hearts? Will you be their hero and friend?

Who Are They?

Life for children in third and fourth grade becomes powerfully demanding, both socially and emotionally. In the United States today, upper elementary students are faced with peer pressures that were common only to high school students just twenty years ago. They are growing physically and emotionally. They are developing a personal sense of independence. Television, radio and the Internet bombard their minds with adult themes and choices. In spite of all this, they are still children and long for the protection and safety of home and family. They are helpful, open and easygoing. They need godly direction, righteous role models and real friends. The key to remember is: *Independence needs guidance and direction.*

Who Is God?

Third and fourth graders are learning to make choices, and they are incorporating their knowledge of God's will into the making of these choices. They are realizing that God has thoughts and feelings and that he wants to be personally involved in their lives.

In addition, these students understand cause and effect. They are learning that their decisions have consequences and are seeing the effects of other people's decisions. They are looking for consistency and safety. God's word now takes on a new dimension; it is becoming the source for making good decisions. This age group desperately wants and needs the goodness, power and protection of God. They are extremely sensitive to right and wrong—especially their own. They have soft consciences that are ready to be fed with God's truth.

Key ideas to remember are: *Our choices make a difference to God. The Bible helps us make good decisions.*

Who Are You?

More than ever before, you, as adults and teachers, are in a position to make lasting impressions. Idealism will soon give way to realism for your students. Your example and integrity will be the background for everything you say. Your life will speak louder than your words. This carries with it an exciting opportunity to inspire, uplift, encourage and prepare their young minds to love God and to live for him. Besides their parents, you are the first line of defense for their souls as they start to grasp the implications of their spirituality. Leave them with memories of God's victories, heroes and miracles that will overshadow the hypocrisy and immorality they see every day. You, like never before, must be Jesus to them.

Key idea to remember is: *The impressions I leave will last a lifetime.*

What to Remember

In about fifteen years, Lord willing, one of your students may be reading these very same words. What will they remember about you? What impression will you leave on them in order to influence *their* next generation? How hard will you pray? Will you be prepared to make *the* difference?

Third and Fourth Grade Lesson

Curriculum Goals

The following diagram represents the cumulative unit goals for the Third and Fourth Grade cycle of curriculum. It builds and reinforces concepts learned in the previous cycles. Every lesson contains *at least* one specific focus from the list below, in addition to a scripture reference, a memory verse and a life application.

The *Generation: Next* curriculum for older school-age students begins in third and fourth grades. This unique and exciting two-year survey of the Bible will offer a solid foundation of Bible history, events andpersonalities. Unlike the primary curriculum, the Third and Fourth Grades will devote the first year to discovering the Old Testament and the second year to discovering the New Testament and God's church today. Students will journey from Genesis to Revelation to God's modern day movement, watching God's power and love unfold before their eyes. The Third and Fourth Grade lessons will provide the vital Biblical background for students who will soon begin their search for a personal relationship with God as they enter their preteen years.

Curriculum Goals	Application to Third and Fourth Graders
Bible Knowledge (This cycle takes a chronological approach to the Bible.)	*THEME:* The Bible is God's word; God chose special men to write the Bible; the Bible is to be obeyed. There is a relationship between Old and New Testaments; major divisions of the Bible are the Law and Prophets and Jesus and Apostles. *CHARACTERS:* Adam and Eve, Cain and Abel, Noah, Abraham and Sarah, Isaac and Jacob, Moses, Joshua, Joseph, David, Saul, Solomon, Esther, Samson, Gideon, Deborah, Samuel, Daniel, Jeremiah, Ezekiel, Elijah, Jesus, Joseph and Mary, Peter, James and John, Paul, Andrew, Thomas, Judas, Ethiopian Eunuch. *EVENTS:* Creation, Flood, Exodus, Ten Command-ments, Wanderings, Birth of Jesus, Temptation of Jesus, Miracles of Nature, Miracles of Healing, Jesus' Crucifixion and Resurrection, Paul and the Early Church, the Church Grows, Pentecost, Cornelius, Eternal Life. *CHRONOLOGY:* Creation, Patriarchs, Exodus, Wander-ings, Promised Land, Judges, Kings, Divided Kingdom, Exile and Return, Major Prophets, Minor Prophets, Gospels, Acts, Letters, Restoration.
Love for God	*CONCEPTS:* God is giving; God takes care of me; God loves me; God made me; God knows all about me; God is not happy when I do wrong; God is happy when I do right; God is our Father; God is powerful; God is patient and kind; God is not easily angered; God has a plan for me; God is always good; I am special and unique to God. God is wise and knows everything; God always knows what is best.

Relationships	*FAMILY:* Obey parents; purpose of family is to serve God; serving and helping in the home; personal responsibility; obeying the first time. *CHURCH:* Obey teachers; be thankful for the church; have best friends in the church; know the church leaders; understand the concept of the body of Christ. *WORLD:* Bring friends to church; give to others; understand world missions. *UNIVERSALS:* Respect, openness, sharing, cooperation, loving others, listening, forgiveness, resolving conflict, responsibility, gratitude.
Character of Christ	*CHARACTERISTICS:* Jesus loves me; Jesus obeyed God and his parents; Jesus was happy and thankful; Jesus' purpose was to serve and to save; Jesus did his best; he loved all people. Jesus was honest, joyful, forgiving and had self-control. *VALUES:* Pleasing God versus pleasing people, judging people by their hearts and not by their appearances; the value of people versus possessions. Jesus' heart: passion, obeying from the heart, avoiding legalism, attitude toward sin, attitude toward the world; Jesus' wisdom.
Prepared to Answer	*CONCEPTS:* God gave us the Bible; the Bible teaches us right from wrong, good from bad, what makes us happy and sad. *MORALITY:* God made us special as a boy or a girl; as disciples we are different from the world. *RELEVANCY OF THE BIBLE:* Not everyone follows the Bible or believes it; not everyone follows all of the Bible. Spiritual responses to violence, drugs, immorality and the media. *APOLOGETICS:* How do we know that the Bible is true? Evidences of the resurrection; plan of salvation versus false doctrines.

Activity Centers

Students will participate in six weekly learning centers: three in the Core Lesson and three in the Supplement.

- Core: Bible Story
- Core: Craft

- Core: Scripture Memory
- Supplement: Life Application
- Supplement: Game
- Supplement: Bible Skills

Bible Story and Life Application

In *Seeds of Faith* (2s and 3s through Second Grade) monthly units alternated between Old and New Testament throughout the year. In the Third and Fourth Grades, the units are designed to provide a continuous overview of the Bible: the first year in the Old Testament and the second year in the New Testament. These lessons have been carefully scripted to help you present them in ways that will make lasting impressions. Students will master key words and concepts as well. In the Supplement Life Application activity center, you will help students look at the Bible Story from a personal perspective and make real-life applications.

Craft

Students will enjoy a variety of craft activities as they are challenged to consider the importance of following instructions and paying attention. Crafts are the tangible memories of important lessons that students will treasure.

Scripture Memory

In the Core Lesson, students continue to master and memorize Bible verses in fun and creative ways. Friends are made through teamwork and cooperative learning. This center attempts not only to help students learn the verse *by* heart, but to take the verse *to* heart as well.

Game

From game shows to charades, students will have lots of fun learning, reviewing and mastering their Bible knowledge. Many games give students the opportunity to work in teams, building and deepening friendships along the way.

Bible Skills

Students sharpen their Bible skills with activities that include speed drills, time lines, map reading, using a concordance and more. Leadership skills are encouraged as students offer help to visiting students or to those who may be less familiar with the Bible.

What's Next?

Students who successfully complete this two-year cycle will have a basic knowledge of Bible history, know the order of the books of the Bible, have a grasp of the differences between Old and New Testament and be able to explain evidences for the inspiration of the Bible. And that is not all. Throughout the two years, students will be challenged to personally think about the consequences of their choices as they develop convictions about sin and personal righteousness. Ultimately, the student who completes this cycle should enter the Preteen class prepared and motivated to seek a personal relationship with God.

27
TEACHING PRETEENS

Clegg & Betty Dyson • Raleigh-Durham, N.C., USA

The most significant thing to appreciate about preteens is that they no longer see themselves as children. What they want to sing or talk about or do is uniquely preteen. Their frustration and impatience with the stuff of children is conveyed in expressions like: "This is lame" or "I'm bored." Most certainly they do not want to be called—or treated like—children.

For most preteens, these years are when questioning authority is the norm. Worldliness is increasingly more attractive. They simultaneously exert their independence and search for their own group.

Preteens experience both physical and emotional changes. Since these changes occur very quickly, often preteens can exhibit strong feelings and emotions. They can be unsettled, uncertain, awkward, insecure and self-conscious. Although each preteen is unique, there are certain characteristics that apply to all preteens at one time or another. Here is a list of the most common characteristics shared by preteens.

- Deep need for group acceptance
- Strong sense of "group spirit"
- Independent and strongly individualistic
- Worry—easily unsettled by difficult circumstances
- Complain when a task is difficult
- Strong feelings and emotions
- Competitiveness
- Investigate, explore and experiment
- Loyalty
- Love brave, daring heroes
- Willing to give their best effort when interested
- Good sense of humor; like to laugh with others, but not have others laugh at them
- Act like children one minute and demand adult privileges the next
- Enjoy joint projects with the opposite sex

- Experience both times of spiritual confidence and times of doubt
- Giggle (girls) and are boisterous (boys)

Spiritual Needs

The preteen years are important years in which spiritual decisions are made that will affect the rest of their lives. Because of this, the preteen ministry is vitally important. Apart from their families, the preteen ministry must serve as their most influential group.

One goal of your ministry should be to use the Kingdom Kids Curriculum to develop in your preteens a spiritual way of thinking. Your role as a teacher is to help these students apply to their own lives key Biblical principles taught in the curriculum: a knowledge of God, Jesus and the Bible. You will ultimately train them to make godly decisions. Since belonging to a peer group is very important to preteens, helping them develop strong relationships in a spiritual group where they feel loved and accepted is equally important. Woven into the Kingdom Kids Curriculum is an intent to build family—to cultivate love, gratitude and respect in the family. No matter what family situation a preteen comes from, through relationships in the church God can make a difference in their lives.

Preteens need brave, daring heroes. Many lessons in the curriculum focus on the great men and women of the Bible. One goal of the curriculum is to help the preteens love men and women of faith and look to *them* as heroes, rather than to the heroes the world has to offer.

Teaching preteens can be challenging since they can act like both young children and young adults. This age group requires your patience and self-control. One way to be victorious is to pray consistently for each of the students by name.

Preteens can express great loyalty. They are willing to take on challenges, to investigate, to ask questions and to work hard. If you give them your time and, more importantly, your heart, the rewards that come from teaching them will be great.

Understanding the Preteen Classroom

Prior to the preteen curriculum, children learn in a center-based environment. They learn and work in small groups as they are taught Bible stories, participate in games and make crafts. The preteen curriculum is very different in that it is built on the group or classroom approach and assumes that a preteen leader is teaching at least some part of the curriculum. For many churches, the preteen ministry is the part of the children's ministry in which the six-month rotation of teachers is replaced by a set leadership chosen by the ministry staff and the children's ministry leaders. This was a conscious part of the Kingdom Kids Curriculum writing. It does not matter if your group of preteens is large or small; group interaction is an important part of a preteen's life and is a key to their learning.

Setting Up Your Classroom

Every church setting is different. In some settings, there may be a large group of preteens. If your group is very large, we suggest dividing it into two classes. Ideally, a class of preteens should have no more than twenty members. Another way to meet the specific needs of your preteens is to occasionally subdivide the class into one group of girls and one group of boys. This method, although helpful in developing relationships and having open discussions, is not recommended for every week.

If you are in a church setting with a very small number of preteens, even two to four, it is important to have a class for these students rather than including them in a younger class. They should know that they are important enough to have a class of their own. The lessons can be modified and adapted to be taught in a smaller setting. A great goal of a class this size would be to pray for the class to grow and for each preteen to bring a friend.

'Generation: Next' Lessons

Preteens need fun, exciting and attractive learning. All of the Kingdom Kids *Generation: Next* preteen lessons are just that—fun, exciting and attractive. To ensure that these lessons come to life, it is your responsibility to read through them prior to teaching them. You should pray, study the scriptures and prepare in advance. Make sure you have everything you will need to effectively teach the lesson and be sure to get help from your assistant teachers. Assign specific jobs to specific people so that all are involved in the teaching process.

When teaching preteens, the manner in which you move from one activity to another can make or break your lesson. Being well prepared and familiar with the materials will help your transition times go well. The lessons are designed to help you because each part of the lesson builds on the previous part. Each lesson ends with a Weekly Challenge. This will help the preteen know how to take what he has learned and apply it to his life. The preteens need your urging and encouragement to carry out these challenges. They also need your praise and encouragement when they are successful with their Weekly Challenges and memory scriptures.

Understanding the Preteen Lesson

Curriculum Goals

The following diagram represents the cumulative unit goals for the preteen cycle of curriculum. It is the cumulative summary of all the goals listed in the previous chapters and introduces areas specific to the needs of preteens.

Curriculum Goals	Application to Preteens
Bible Knowledge	**CHARACTERS:** Adam and Eve, Cain and Abel, Noah, Abraham and Sarah, Isaac and Jacob, Moses, Joshua, Joseph, David, Saul, Solomon, Esther, Samson, Gideon, Deborah, Samuel, Daniel, Jeremiah, Ezekiel, Elijah, Jesus, Joseph and Mary, Peter, James and John, Paul, Andrew, Thomas, Judas, Temptation of Jesus, Ethiopian Eunuch. **EVENTS:** Creation, Flood, Exodus, Ten Commandments, Wanderings, Birth of Jesus, Miracles of Nature, Miracles of Healing, Jesus' Crucifixion and Resurrection, Paul and the Early Church, the Church Grows, Pentecost, Cornelius, Eternal Life. **CHRONOLOGY:** Creation, Patriarchs, Exodus, Wanderings, Promised Land, Judges, Kings, Divided Kingdom, Exile and Return, Major Prophets, Minor Prophets, Gospels, Acts, Letters, Restoration. **ADDITIONAL:** Emphasis on women in the Bible, children of the Bible.

Love for God	**Concepts:** God is giving; God takes care of me; God loves me; God made me; God knows all about me; God is not happy when I do wrong; God is happy when I do right; God is our Father; God is powerful; God is patient and kind; God is not easily angered; God has a plan for me; God is always good; I am special and unique to God; God is wise and knows everything; God always knows what is best. God protects, heals and can do the impossible; Jesus is divine.
Relationships	**Family:** Obeying parents; purpose of family is serving God; serving and helping in the home; taking personal responsibility; obeying the first time; having a sense of mission; being unified in purpose. **Church:** Obeying teachers; being thankful for the church; having best friends in the church; knowing the leaders; understanding the concept of the body. **World:** Bringing friends to church; giving to others; understanding world missions; having vision for their own lives; overcoming a victim mentality. **Universals:** Respect, openness, sharing, cooperation, loving others, listening, forgiveness, resolving conflict, responsibility, gratitude; not being critical.
Character of Christ	**Characteristics:** Jesus loves me; Jesus obeyed God and his parents; Jesus was happy and thankful; Jesus' purpose was to serve and to save. Jesus did his best; he loved all people. Jesus was honest, joyful, forgiving and had self-control. **Values:** Pleasing God versus pleasing people; judging people by their hearts and not by their appearances; the value of people versus possessions. **Jesus' heart:** Passionate; obeying from the heart; avoiding legalism; attitude toward sin; attitude toward the world; Jesus' wisdom. **Balance of Traits:** toughness and gentleness; perfect human; had a "tough" love; Jesus can relate to our lives; Jesus defies all levels of prejudice.

Prepared to Answer	**CONCEPTS:** God gave us the Bible; the Bible teaches us right from wrong, good from bad, what makes us happy and sad. **MORALITY:** God made us special as a boy or a girl; as disciples we are different from the world. **RELEVANCY OF THE BIBLE:** Not everyone follows the Bible or believes it; not everyone follows all of the Bible. Spiritual responses to violence, drugs, immorality and the media. **APOLOGETICS:** How do we know that the Bible is true? Evidences of the resurrection; plan of salvation versus false doctrines; why discipleship? Morality and ethics.

A preteen lesson contains both a Core and Supplement Lesson and a reproducible section. The Core Lesson appears first, followed by the Supplement Lesson. Included in both lessons are four major sections: Lesson at a Glance, Getting Ready, Getting into God's Word and Getting It to Others.

Lesson at a Glance offers a quick way for you to get an overview of what the lesson entails and how it relates to the overall unit. Getting Ready includes all the preparation necessary to teach a lesson and any activities that occur prior to the start of class. Getting into God's Word contains the Biblically based lesson and other related activities. Getting It to Others involves activities, including a Weekly Challenge, which help the preteens apply the lesson to their own lives and the lives of others.

Following the Core and Supplement Lesson are Reproducible Pages. These pages are to be copied and are referenced in the lessons where they apply. A Reproducible Page might be a scripture memory verse, a story, a chart or a worksheet that will be used in a lesson.

The students will also receive a Quiet Time Journal (*Extreme Life I* and *II*), which is designed to complement the lesson each week. Each day they will be given a scripture, a question and a prayer suggestion for the day that comprise a follow-up to the Core and Supplement Lessons. They will learn to be consistent in their times with God and to apply the principles and facts that they are learning in class.

Preparing your lesson with the Kingdom Kids Curriculum is time-consuming to be sure, but it is well worth the time you spend. And if you don't spend both time *and* energy to prepare, the preteens will realize it. They will not feel special or respected, and they probably will not respond enthusiastically to your attempts to lead them.

Be "out of yourself" and give them your best. You have an incredible opportunity to influence these children for the rest of their lives. They will go into the young teens after your class...a time when they will begin to make the most important life decision they will ever make. Make it your goal to set them up to choose life, to choose to make Jesus their Lord.

28
A POWERFUL PRETEEN MINISTRY

Clegg & Betty Dyson • Raleigh-Durham, N.C., USA

The preteen years are a time of great change and growth. Developmentally, preteens are coming into their own. They are trying to figure out who they are and how they want others to view them. They face peer pressure at school and in their neighborhoods. They are beginning to make their own decisions about things that matter. At the same time the worldliness is increasingly more attractive and inviting. Since preteens have very little experience from which to draw and since parents and other disciples cannot be with them all the time, they must be taught how to make the best choices.

A Vital Ministry

Many adult disciples hold the view that a preteen ministry is a holding ground between a children's ministry and a teen ministry. This view is not true. Many of our churches have a large number of preteens and have had a preteen ministry for a number of years. They have seen the crucial need for a powerful program for the preteens, or else the preteens will find other outlets for their energies. Many preteens make their decisions about God, the church and the Bible long before they reach the teen ministry. The preteen ministry is perhaps the ministry that has the most powerful influence in leading young teens to Christ.

In order to make a positive impact on preteens, the preteen ministry should have three primary objectives:

1. *Present Jesus, God and the church in a manner that is exciting, inspiring, fun and practical.* In order to accomplish this, we strongly recommend that classroom space be provided for the preteens, both for Sunday and midweek classes. Logistical challenges or budget issues, like a lack of classroom space or teachers, should not be the

deciding factor in whether or not to provide the preteens with an opportunity to learn. For most preteens, sitting in the adult classes or sitting in on the Sunday sermons is both frustrating and boring, which will become their memory of church. Lessons need to be geared to the preteens' level in order to be interesting for them. They need to see how they can use the Bible in their real-life situations: family, school, neighborhood, sports teams, hobbies and activities. The *Generation: Next* curriculum for preteens has been written so that the Bible will be of practical use to them.

An important element in any preteen ministry is making Jesus a hero in the preteens' eyes. He must be as real and impressive as any current sports or entertainment hero that the world holds up. To encourage the students to make Jesus their hero, it is important to select preteen ministry leaders and teachers who are fun-loving and can relate well to the preteens. These adult leaders must be spiritually strong and members of the church for no less than six months. These adults need to connect through an understanding and awareness of what is "in" with preteens. An adult may not have this connection when they are first selected to work with this age group, but they must be the kind of disciples who are willing to learn and be taught by their students as to what is "in" for preteens.

Not every spiritually strong disciple will make a great preteen teacher. For instance, preteens often relate to each other and to adults through appearance. An adult does not necessarily have to dress like the preteens do, but a sense of style is very helpful. Preteens are very conscious of weight, dress, personality and the like as a measure of who they allow to influence them. While to many of us this is "worldly," to them it is normal. At this age they need to be able to relate to their teachers more so than in younger classes. How we look does matter to the preteens, especially when they are bringing their friends to church with them. The goal of preteen leaders and teachers is to make the gospel attractive to those they are trying to reach with the love of God. Here are some helpful tips that will help preteen leaders and teachers.

- If you are overweight, lose the extra pounds (exercise and get in shape).
- If you have bad breath, freshen it.

- If your hair is greasy, wash it.
- If your clothes are dated, toss them.
- If your musical knowledge is limited to the "Oldies" or classical, listen to your preteens' favorite radio stations.

2. *Create an arena in which preteens can build best-friend relationships that will help keep them faithful as they grow up together.* The preteen ministry must provide opportunities for the preteens to hang out together. A monthly, churchwide devotional is an excellent opportunity for preteens to get to know other preteens from around the church. For churches with a large number of preteens, regions can conduct monthly devotionals. These devotionals can be held on Saturday mornings or Sunday afternoons. The following is a brief list of devotional ideas:

- Brief lessons on Jesus and other Bible heroes, such as David, Daniel, Jacob, Esther, Deborah, Ruth, etc. Follow these lessons with small group discussions or activities that relate to the lesson. You can also have a big, group game that teaches unity and good sportsmanship.

- Brief lessons on loving and helping the poor. These could be followed by planning fund-raisers to help the poor. For example, plan a skating party at a local skating rink. Charge a dollar or two above the admission fee, and donate the extra money to a project for the poor.

- Lessons in which the group is divided into boys and girls. Have a lesson for the boys entitled "A Man of God" and one for the girls entitled "A Woman of God." Afterward, the boys can play a game related to the lesson, and the girls can learn about hair styling and clothing from a disciple who is a professional in the field.

Disciples who have led devotionals for years have found that a twenty-minute lesson works best with the preteens' attention span. The fun activity is very important after the lesson because preteens need to move and interact with each other. Most Bible bookstores offer a good selection of books containing icebreaker activities and great game ideas for preteens. These books are helpful in planning preteen devotionals.

Great activities are essential in helping preteens build enduring friendships. Be careful not to center all your activities around athletics and competition. Some preteens are not athletic and may feel they do not fit in if most of your activities are sports oriented. Variety is a key part of making things fun. Whatever is chosen needs to be done excellently. It needs to be organized and planned thoroughly. If athletic events are selected, emphasis needs to be placed on participation, not on competing to win.

A churchwide preteen Olympics is a great activity for spring. Each team should have its own identifying color. The Olympics can promote unity and friendship among the preteens. Preteens can compete by regions. Indoor games, track and field events, volleyball and basketball are just a few possible areas of competition. You could even include some relay competitions that do not require exceptional athletic ability. Ribbons and medals can be awarded to the first-, second- and third-place winners in each competition. Then award a trophy to the team that wins the most points. You can also give groups a ribbon for having the best cheer, the best team spirit and the most creative banner or flag. In fact, make sure that every team wins some award (even if it is the "Brightest Smiles Award") so all preteens go home feeling successful. To ensure that no group is overlooked, have a representative of each group on the judging committee.

Parties are also important friendship builders. These can be planned for a Sunday class or a region. Here are some ideas: Biblical costume parties, Thanksgiving feasts with thank-you devotionals, Christmas parties, monthly birthday parties, bowling parties, picnics and outdoor sports parties.

Many churches offer preteen summer camps lasting from three to four days to as long as a week. With an adequate number of adults to serve as counselors and chaperones, camp can be a life-changing experience for a preteen. So much can be accomplished at camp: many brief Bible lessons, messages from guest speakers, discussion groups, sports, swimming, arts and crafts, great fellowship, entertainment, talent shows and more. Camp can be an incredible memory for a preteen. Check with other ministries who have already had experience with conducting camps so you can learn from them. If you only have a few preteens, you might want to check into sending them to a larger ministry's camp.

3. *Help the preteens to develop faith in God, Jesus and the Bible, and to make godly decisions for their lives based on the Bible.* This goal should be woven through the entire preteen ministry. This can be accomplished by asking questions to make the preteens think and then respond. Preteen teachers need to be careful not to just give information from the Bible, but to give the preteens the opportunity to think and reason, using the Bible as the standard. This is particularly true of children who have been around the church for some time.

The preteen ministry should have a close relationship with the teen and campus ministries. Strong teen and college disciples should be invited to speak to the preteens from time to time. This allows the disciples to share about their lives and how they make decisions based on their faith in God, their relationships with him and their knowledge of his word. The preteens need the encouragement of seeing and learning from faithful teen disciples. This also meets their need to have heroes. Relatable teens and college students are great role models for preteens.

By being personally open, the teacher helps the preteens to understand how adult disciples make godly decisions. The preteen teachers can share about their daily walk with God, their relationships with other brothers and sisters and their personal involvement in making disciples. They can also share how God has helped them to overcome weaknesses and turn those weaknesses into strengths.

An inspiring preteen ministry is a vital ministry of any church. It should never be optional. This ministry will have a most powerful impact in leading the next generation to Christ. Do not underestimate its influence and significance!

Contributors

SUE ANDERSON serves as the children's ministry leader for the Washington D.C. church and helped to oversee the writing of three preteen units in the Kingdom Kids Curriculum. She also is an operation director for the American Commonwealth Region's summer camp.

AL BAIRD and his wife, Gloria, serve as world sector leaders for the Law and Media World Sector of the International Churches of Christ.

JOY BODZIOCH and her husband, Adam, direct the children's ministry for the San Francisco Church of Christ.

JOHN BRINGARDNER, ESQ. is the general counsel for the International Churches of Christ.

RON AND LINDA BRUMLEY serve as elder and wife for the Seattle Church of Christ. Linda currently oversees the children's ministries in Seattle and in the Northwest churches.

JOYCE CONN assists in overseeing and training all of the children's ministry leaders for the New York City Church of Christ. She also served on the advisory committee for the Kingdom Kids Curriculum.

ROB DAVIS and his wife, Tess, have served as assistant children's ministry leaders and as exceptional lead teachers and assistants for the North Region of the Boston church.

CLEGG AND BETTY DYSON served for many years as children's ministry leaders in the Boston Church of Christ and they were members of the advisory committee for the Kingdom Kids Curriculum. They currently are part of the Triangle Church in North Carolina.

KIM EVANS serves as a women's ministry leader in the Greater Philadelphia Church of Christ.

GAIL EWELL serves as the women's ministry leader for the San Francisco Church of Christ and for the NET (New Media, Exceptional Children and Technology) World Sector of the International Churches of Christ. Gail and her husband, Russ, have developed an outstanding ministry for children with special needs.

JOE FARMER serves on the staff of the New York City church, along with his wife, Margie, and they work with the children's ministry, preteen ministry and spiritual recovery ministry. They also served on the advisory committee for the Kingdom Kids Curriculum.

GORDON FERGUSON serves as an elder in the Boston Church of Christ and as a kingdom teacher who has authored numerous books. He served as the chairman of the advisory committee for the Kingdom Kids Curriculum.

THERESA FERGUSON is a women's ministry leader in the Boston Church of Christ. She serves alongside her husband Gordon in his role as an elder and was also a member of the advisory committee.

JORGE AND DEBBIE GARCIA-BENGOCHEA, members of the South Florida Church of Christ, are the educational directors for the Central and South America World Sector of the International Churches of Christ. Debbie was a writer for the preteen portion of the Kingdom Kids Curriculum.

VICKI JACOBY and her husband, Douglas, serve as directors of education for the British Commonwealth World Sector of the International Churches of Christ. They have oversight of staff training, members' education and children's ministry in all British Commonwealth churches.

KATIE LABOMBARD was the preschool editor for the Kingdom Kids Curriculum and served on the advisory committee. Currently, she serves as the curriculum editor with DPI.

BARRY AND NANCY LAMB serve as children's ministry leaders for the London church and oversee children's ministry for the United Kingdom International Churches of Christ.

AMBY MURPHY and her husband, Tim, have served as the children's ministry leaders in the South Region of the Boston church for four years. She was the school-age editor of the Kingdom Kids Curriculum and served on the advisory committee

JAYNE RICKER serves as the children's ministry leader for the San Diego Church of Christ and for the Southwest family of International Churches of Christ. She helped to oversee the development of the Kingdom Kids Curriculum for first and second graders.

DARLA ROWE serves as children's ministry leader, as well as working beside her husband, Woody, elder and administrator for the Nashville

Church. She helped to oversee the development of the Kingdom Kids Curriculum for two and three year olds.

Lois Schmitt serves as the director of children's ministry for the Atlanta Church of Christ. She helped develop the Kingdom Kids Curriculum for the two and three year olds.

Ben and Beth Weast oversee the children's, preteen and teen ministries for the Triangle Church of Christ. They helped write several of the preteen lessons for the Kingdom Kids Curriculum and several family devotionals for As for Me and My House.

Larry and Lea Wood serve as children's ministry leaders for the Northwest Region of the Boston church. Larry is also managing editor for DPI. Together, he and Lea edited The Heart of a Champion for Kids.

Sheridan Wright serves as elder/evangelist in the New York City church and along with his wife, oversees the children's ministry, preteen ministry and the spiritual recovery ministry. Additionally, he served as a member of the advisory committee for the Kingdom Kids Curriculum.

Debbie Wright serves as a women's ministry leader in the New York City church, and along with her husband, oversees the children's ministry, preteen ministry and the spiritual recovery ministry. She also served as a member of the advisory committee for the Kingdom Kids Curriculum.

Who Are We?

Discipleship Publications International (DPI) began publishing in 1993. We are a nonprofit Christian publisher affiliated with the International Churches of Christ, committed to publishing and distributing materials that honor God, lift up Jesus Christ and show how his message practically applies to all areas of life. We have a deep conviction that no one changes life like Jesus and that the implementation of his teaching will revolutionize any life, any marriage, any family and any singles household.

Since our beginning we have published nearly 100 titles; plus we have produced a number of important, spiritual audio products. More than one million volumes have been printed, and our works have been translated into more than a dozen languages—international is not just a part of our name! Our books are shipped regularly to every inhabited continent.

To see a more detailed description of our works, find us on the World Wide Web at www.dpibooks.org. You can order books by calling 1-888-DPI-BOOK twenty-four hours a day. From outside the US, call 781-937-3883, ext. 231 during Boston-area business hours.

We appreciate the hundreds of comments we have received from readers. We would love to hear from you. Here are other ways to get in touch:

Mail: DPI, One Merrill St., Woburn, MA 01801
E-mail: dpibooks@icoc.org

Find Us on the
World Wide Web

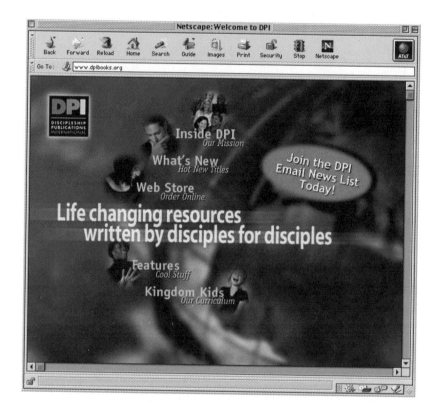

www.dpibooks.org
1-888-DPI-BOOK
outside US: 781-937-3883 x231